FIVE DOLLARS IN CHANGE

The Controversial Stories of My Life

Manuel L. Luz
As told to his niece,
Editha Luz Asuncion
Second Edition with commentary
from his son, Manuel A. Luz Jr.

Contact: manuel@manuelluz.com

ISBN-13: 9781234567890
ISBN-10: 1477123456

Library of Congress Control Number: 2018675309
Printed in the United States of America

CONTENTS

Title Page

Copyright

About This Second Edition

Preface: My Failings 1

1. The Innocent Teenager 3

2. My Military Experience 14

3. Labor Involvement 28

4: If You Do Not Work, You Shall Not Eat 47

5. The Filipino Community Connection 63

6. Political Connections 80

7. The Road to Family Contentment 101

8. Life Stories 126

9. My Community Service Involvement 148

ABOUT THIS SECOND EDITION

When I was a little kid, I loved going into my dad's office to watch him work. In those days, my dad had a side business as a tax preparer, notary public, and real estate broker, and he ran his office out of our converted one-car garage. Fascinated, I would sit for what felt like hours in the chair beside his desk and quietly watch him work. And the thing I loved the most was when he operated the old gun-metal green mechanical adding machine that sat on his desk. As he punched in each number, the adding machine would respond with a "Click-clack-click-clack-click," and then as he pulled on its single massive arm, it would punctuate the racket with a boisterous, "Kachoonka!" I remember the rolls and rolls of white paper that cascaded to the floor like ribbons in a ticker tape parade. It was like magic, only better. Cause it was Dad doing it.

It's funny that a memory like that would have such a profound impact on me as an eight-year-old boy.

The older I get, the more I believe that the true life-legacy you leave behind are the stories your children tell their children about you. It is in these family stories—sometimes embellished and tinted by the passing of time—that one's true character and heritage can truly be discovered. So much of what I know about our family history was told to me by my parents at the dinner table. My mom and dad sharing stories about living in the Philippines during World War II, or working the canneries in Alaska, or picking crops in Idaho, or cooking white rice over an open fire, or working the early shift at Soledad Prison, or the swing shift at the Memorial Hospital. These are the stories that form the backdrop of our lives.

My father was an unusual man, filled with equal parts of ambition and intelligence and integrity and wisdom. He was one of the Manong Generation, those Filipino immigrants who came to the United States during the 1920s-1930s. Manong is an Ilokano (northern Filipino regional dialect) term which means, "older brother," and indeed, my father was the older brother statesman for many of his generation and those who followed. This generation suffered many unique and harrowing indignities and prejudices specific to the Filipinos of that time, and they responded with bravery and fortitude to the challenge. Those of us from succeeding generations owe these pioneers deep gratitude and admiration.

In a lifetime of knowing my father, I have never known him to hold a grudge, never harbor any bitterness for life, never let the cruelty and injustices of life beat him. In all his roles—as a father, husband, employee, politician, civic leader, business owner, and friend—he always demonstrated a quiet strength, one which turned negatives into positives, setbacks into opportunities, enemies into allies. It was a strength born from uncommon ambition and a great sense of moral obligation. It was a strength which conquered the discrimination and hatred and denied opportunities that would defeat lesser men.

This autobiography is the result of many years of encouraging my father to write down the many anecdotes and reminiscences he and my om told us over the years. And we're so very grateful that he did. For these stories—told by a first-generation Filipino immigrant—are historically important, sociologically consequential, and personally revealing. Thankfully, my dad completed his memoirs in 1995, six years before his passing on February 12, 2001, and fifteen years before the passing of my mom on February 2, 2010.

A few notes to help you read this book. These memoirs were originally published for my family only; This second edition is released at the request of others who found his writings not just interesting but important to the story of the Filipino in America. All words are essentially those of my father, except for edits to clarify the meaning. All the footnotes are mine, except when annotated as an Author's Note. (In general, my words are in italics.) I hope my footnotes, both historical and personal, help provide context for these memoirs, especially to the younger generations. May these writings magnify your understanding of the Filipino in America, and by inference, your understanding of your own identity in the world.

—MANUEL A. LUZ JR.

PREFACE: MY FAILINGS

Service has always been in my blood and in my heart. It is my reason for living. It is the compelling force behind all my activities. It is the singular medium through which I show my pride and appreciation of my existence in this universe. Under this premise, I allowed myself to get involved in countless voluntary activities and services over the years. Not that I am a volunteer bug, for in almost all my social volunteer services, I was asked or was chosen to serve. When I see tears of joy in the eyes of those who were served, when I hear words of gratitude from recipients of my services, my heart always grows a little with a sigh of contentment, and I feel that my existence is fulfilled. I feel no regrets whatsoever—I have paid in part my reason for living.

I feel, however, that my life has been a failure—that there is no reason for jubilation. I was born with the inherited appellation of "Luz," which means “light.” I was born in a small community called "Laoag," which also translates to “light.” I attempted to become an electrical engineer, which in a sense is “light,” (this study was abruptly curtailed by the Great Depression). At one time, I was imbued with the desire to go to the ministry—another form of “light.”[1] I completed the prescribed courses at a college of law—another form of “light.”[2] My life's pride lies then in the numerous volunteer services rendered unto my people and to all peoples, however significant they may be.

I have been asked on several occasions when vacationing in the Republic of the Philippines what course of study I successfully acquired in the United States.[3] My ready reply to their uncalled-for question was, "BSPL," a degree which took them agape for proper elucidation. I conferred myself that degree: “Bachelor of Science in Practical Living.” When I retired at the young age of 83, I then retired not only from one line of work, I completely and irrevocably retired as a jack-of-all-trades.

In the year 1926, I landed in Seattle, Washington, wet behind the ears, not knowing a single individual, faced by the mysteries and beauty of a new land, with the difficulty of understanding the language, the mores, the customs, and the traditions—and with a mere pittance of five dollars in my pocket. Unknown and bewildered, I had no alternative but to survive. As time has shown, I was able to readjust myself to these strange conditions, surmount a lifetime's worth of obstacles and live and serve (my middle name) to this age. So I suppose I should be proud of this insignificant success; my investment of five dollars has grown to at least fifty dollars. A real feat, indeed!

1. THE INNOCENT TEENAGER

Most teenagers face the typical challenges of adolescence—social acceptance, scholastics, technology, identity. My father grew up in the Philippines, between the Great War and the Great Depression. For him, adolescence was about survival, about providing for his family, about finding a way out of poverty and hopelessness. I think it's important for all young people, especially those of Filipino descent, to understand this part of our shared heritage—for this is what made and motivated our forefathers to leave their homelands and make the lonely trek to the United States to make a better life for themselves and their families.

Laoag City, Republic of the Philippines, is a thriving and growing community situated in the northwestern corner of the island of Luzon. It is an economic, commercial, and education center in the northern Philippines. Transportation companies converge there, it is the seat of the Provincial Government, and it is the locale for four complete universities, trade and normal schools, and various schools of technical learning.

It was not like this, however, decades and scores ago, when I was born on June 17, 1906, in a bamboo-nipa hut my father built. An overgrown village then, but it was proudly designated the capital city of Ilocos Norte. It also boasted the only high school in the entire province, with no institutions of higher learning.

I came into this cruel world greeted by demoralizing poverty and amidst very depressing, meager circumstances. I was one of seven children: three brothers older that I, and two sisters and a brother younger. I have no memories of the elder brothers, nor had I even been given the liberty of knowing their names, for they succumbed as infants. The gospel truth was my parents regarded me as a miracle sibling, for l survived the same infirmities and circumstances as the others. Their names were never mentioned again in the household because it brought so much untold misery and bad memories to our very caring parents. Our household consisted of: Father, Marcelo Flores Luz; mother, Dominga Maximo Lorenzo (maiden name); sisters, Salvacion Lorenzo Luz and Generosa Lorenzo Luz; and brother, Lucas Lorenzo Luz.[4] The family on my father's lineage is related to the Flores, Santellas, Orjeles and Lagasca clans. We are kinfolk maternally to the Lorenzo, Maximo, Pedro, and Ancheta families. As with many Filipino families then, the authentic nature of these relationships was never explicitly elaborated. I only accepted as truth.

My father—an unassuming but understanding individual —was a humble laborer, who spent his entire adult life as a messenger-helper at the local postal service. He was soft spoken, and rarely expressed his deep feelings or decided opinions on past or present issues. Not that he was totally illiterate, but as he repeatedly advised me, "Keep your thoughts and opinions to free yourself from trouble." He was an honest, decent, lawabiding person, who devoted most of his time for the good and welfare of his family. He was always willing and ready to deny himself to serve his family.

My loving mother never learned to read or write and could not even sign her signature. She was, however, an astute and clever individual. Her most prominent attribute was her discerning ability to perceive what she observed and heard. We, her children, could hardly hide anything from her sensibilities. To augment the meager income from father's employment, she operated a small *sari-sari*[5] store at a makeshift shop under our humble bamboo house. I spent days watching her transact business, and to my memory, no one ever succeeded in outwitting her.

My loving parents saw in us, their offspring, the realization of their deep-rooted dreams of a better life, by encouraging us to study and acquire a good education.[6] So at a very early age, I learned my ABCs under the watchful eye and tutelage of an aunt, a loving sister of Father. She diligently coached me and taught me how to read and write. Understand that the family could not afford the luxury of a pencil, much less writing paper. To the family, these items belonged to the rich and the affluent. But we did a lot of improvisation. Banana leaves were plentiful and bamboo sticks were abundantly free. We carved the bamboo sticks into the shape of pencils and cut the banana leaves to use as writing paper. It served our purpose beautifully. Proudly, I can tell the world I learned to write with the two B's: Bamboo and Banana.

◆ ◆ ◆

I grew up like other children of the town, our neighborhood, or perhaps anywhere in the Philippines. So as a boy, I loved sports and games. This yen to play was generated partly by the prevalence of sport facilities in our neighborhood, which were built and sanctioned by our parents and neighbors. There was a volleyball court, a popular sport in our day, a tennis court, the "rings," or *argulla,* and we even had a trapeze, the *trupecio*. In the home of one of our advisers and benefactors was a ping-pong table which was available to the kids on the block. Streetball, or sandlot softball, was also a favorite past-time.

There were neighborhood clubs all over the city, not the kind of gangs that caused trouble, but clubs organized to build character and sportsmanship and inspirations for building community spirit. Our club was titled "The Junior Council of Laoag," meaning we discussed issues not exclusively for club members but issues affecting the whole community.

There were friendly rivalries among the different clubs in the city. Challenges in volleyball or softball were common;[7] debating and oratorical contests prevailed; and during the Town Fiesta, the clubs would vie to present the best skits and plays to augment the common *comedia*, with the blessing of the city. By building their own floats, these clubs participated in parades on the Fourth of July or other patriotic holidays. I do believe that with all these programs, the kids of my generation did not have the leisure time for mischief and misbehaving. I preferred to waste my time playing games than to learn the basics of education. Like others, I made my own toys, invented my own games, and enjoyed sports.

When I initially tried to enroll in public school, I suffered the indignity of being unceremoniously rejected. During that period, it was not unusual to have children over ten years old start attending first grade. The number of students in a class and the number of classes was limited. Hence some of the applicants for admission would be advised to go home with the reassuring advice to try again the following year.

Now in order to find out whether a child was ready for school, a simple test was employed: the prospective student was required to raise the right hand upward, arch it over his head, and touch the left ear. Being one of the smallest of the enrollees, I utterly failed to pass the rudimentary and fundamental tests. I could not for the love of life accomplish that trick. Having failed to accomplish this acrobatic test, I was, to no surprise, advised to spend another year out of school. It was a tremendous shock to me; I was broken-hearted, crying and sobbing.

After some time, I was able to compose myself. I braced myself, and with pride and some bravado, I confronted the seemingly dictatorial teacher. I dared her to test me against any of the chosen in reading and writing. The teacher, no doubt, was shocked by my daring confrontation. After my continued insistence, she finally granted my pleadings. Directing me to the blackboard, she handed me chalk and an eraser, and in front of the chosen, ordered me to write my name, which I wrote perfectly, then dictated me to scribble other words and even short sentences. Needless for me to attest, I became her star pupil, for it became later evident that most of the pupils didn't even know the alphabet.

Another incident in my young life that sticks to my memory happened during school registration on my third year at the Laoag Central School. There were then no prior registrations. Pupils reported on the first day of school and were divided into groups, with a teacher assigned to a group or class. We were ordered to find seats and after control was established, the teacher proceeded to list the pupils going from one desk to another. I found myself sitting amongst strangers. When the young lad sitting immediately behind me was called, he stood up and quietly pronounced that his name was Manuel Luz. Not by design but by fate, I was the next to be asked my name. Shyly, I stood up and proudly shouted, "My name is Manuel Luz." The teacher could not hide her anger, above the uproar and amusement of the student body. The teacher shouting above the laughter repeatedly asked us our names, thinking I presume, we were doing it in jest, but we stuck to the gospel truth that we were both christened, Manuel Luz. Being the smaller of the Manuels, the confused teacher tried hard to expatriate me to another room. Her sincere efforts to disassociate us ended in her total disappointment. The mix-up was finally settled by inserting our middle initials. He became Manuel B and I became Manuel L. The confusion and fun didn't end there, however. On numerous occasions, the teacher would forget the different initials and both of the Manuels would stand up to answer questions, sometimes with conflicting points of view.

In those years, Philippine elementary schools included industrial arts in their curriculums. The primary grades (1-4) were mandated to basket-weaving and/or fan-making for the boys, with sewing and lace-making for the girls. In the intermediate grades (5-6) the boys had the option to engage in gardening, or chicken or pig raising. In my fifth grade, I opted for gardening and in the upper classes, I choose chicken raising. I selected these courses with the ultimate goal of helping the family. One full year of gardening instruction and supervision on school farms had given me the background to till my own garden. An open lot across our humble bamboo hut became my private garden where I grew and cultivated various vegetables. My entire family, of course, helped tirelessly in the venture and the immediate neighborhood also helped in the consumption.

While my gardening experience was in progress, I chose poultry raising as my school project. Thus, the family was assured of fresh vegetables from the garden, and occasionally or on special days, chicken and eggs for the table. These little luxuries were not destined to last forever. Eventually, the owner of my garden plot decided to construct his home on it and the chickens perished by recurrent uncontrollable pestilences.

My family didn't have the material luxuries of easy living.[8] We knew the pangs of hunger to the point that we could not sleep, our stomachs constantly crying for sustenance. We experienced many days when two meager meals were luxuries. I also vividly remember that most of the clothing the family possessed were not the store variety. We had a weaving loom under our humble home where the family clan—including me—wove panels of cotton cloth, which were made into our clothes. From the cotton balls spun into threads and woven into materials, to the cutting and sewing of clothing, indeed, such is the gospel truth. Ln spite of this lack of convenience, my parents continually instilled upon us, their siblings, the importance of acquiring an education.

I clearly and vividly remember that the first store-bought clothing I ever wore was the high school ROTC uniform mandated by the government and high schools. All male students were required—without exception—to take this course. Since I had met all requirements and qualifications, I was commissioned a captain, assigned to command a company and occasionally command a full battalion on parades and competitions. This para-military experience—supplemented by my love of mathematics, algebra, geometry and physics—instilled in me the desire to seek appointment into a military academy. This secret dream for a military career slowly faded away when it became evident that who-you-know and not what-you-know accounted entirely in the appointments.

There was another incident in my high school days that surely needs telling. This particular event happened during school opening. Matriculation fees, an invention of the powers in our educational system, were conceived, designed and strictly enforced. Added to this burden was the purchase of school supplies and books by the students. To protest this burdensome requirement, I organized a bunch of my friends and urged them to pay this unjust taxation in small coins, in this case, Philippine centavos. The Philippine centavo was then the size of a US quarter, metallic and heavy.

We lined up for registration, bags of coins on hand, and as we were called, we dumped those bags of big centavos at the registrar's desk. Of course, our actions caused pandemonium amongst the teachers, the students, and the principal. Cool heads finally prevailed, and the principal calmly and wisely requested us to collect our booty and come back with lighter denominations. We may have lost our cause, but the surprise protest didn't fall on deaf ears! As a consequence of my organizing and leading the protest against the school matriculation fiasco, I was dubbed by classmates as the "Philosopher of Section Seven," a reputation that spread among the student body.

As is universal, students would cram for final examinations. At that time, all exams were of the essay type; no true-or-false kinds of test were instituted. So during finals, my house always became a review school. Students I never knew came and participated in these study sessions. My great peeve then was that I could not indulge in sports and play. These students never asked me to review with them. They would approach my mother, who would assure them that I would be there—and I could not defy or neglect her promise. These routines were continued through my high school days. During school days, there were many nights I would be confined to the house for many students would be there for individual assistance.

There were a couple of semi-retarded lads in my neighborhood. It was my desire to voluntarily tutor them in the fundamentals of reading and writing until they were fully prepared to enter public schools.

I was not a very serious student. I never crammed for exams or studied with the midnight oil, but I got by school okay. In history for instance, I would learn my assignment on my way walking to school.

As the eldest living offspring of the family, it was incumbent upon me to improve the financial situation of the clan. So as a young lad, healthy and sturdy, between school and play, I had to find ways and means to earn a few pennies. Picture a growing lad in the elementary grades peddling drinking water to the affluent and to families living far from waler sources. With a pair of five-gallon cans carried on a bamboo pole totting them blocks away—for a mere cent a can! During vacations or when there was no school, I would be swinging a pick, shoveling, or mixing cement for the town's road improvement projects. When I was in high school, an uncle—a husband of my mother's sister and music—gave me music lessons[9] and eventually encouraged me to join his band in some of their performances. It was the practice in those days that occasions like christenings, weddings and funerals were served with appropriate music, such as what my uncle's band could furnish. I earned more from these activities than from road construction or other demeaning endeavors. I also learned the real value of money, so I started to save some with the postal service, a savings which became handy when I decided to seek my fortune abroad.

◆ ◆ ◆

During my sophomore year in high school, I, along with some of my buddies, learned that if we could pass the government Civil Service exams, it would be easier lo land government employment. A number of us decided to challenge the demanding tests. But there was a catch. To participate, you had to possess a valid personal *cedula*, a sort of identification for those who have attained the age of maturity.[10] My father, realizing my predicament, produced for me the authentic *cedula*. I took the second-grade Civil Service exam and was proud to have hurdled it in my first attempt. With this second-grade Civil Service eligible credential, I was offered several different jobs away from home. My parents, however, adamantly objected to having me distance myself from the family. They persistently egged me on to best finish high school, the highest educational institution in Ilocos Norte. I, therefore, continued my studies and graduated in the top ten of the Class of 1925.

Math had always been my favorite subject, beginning in the primary grades when I was selected to compete against pupils from all over the province during the Provincial Fair. In fact, when the math instructor was unable to attend classes, I would more or less substitute so that the class and I could work and learn together. In many cases, I was exempted from taking final exams.

It was a forgone conclusion that I could not financially afford to pursue a higher education. Universities, colleges, and schools of higher learning were all located in Manila. My alternative was to land a paying job, which was like looking for a needle in a haystack. I finally landed a position as a teacher in a remote and isolated barrio of the municipality, a village shunned by experienced teachers. It did not take me long to find the fundamental reason why teachers refused an assignment to this barrio school, a single room structure occupied by students, grades one to four.

One day, I had a very tiring and hair-raising experience, an unforeseen accident. After classes were dismissed, I headed to the *poblacion*, riding proudly on my only means of transportation—a gentle horse. Following unchartered trails on lonely and hilly terrain, my gentle four-legged friend stepped on a grass-covered hole, throwing me tumbling down, with a foot stuck on the stirrup. It was indeed a miracle that the horse decided not to gallop or run. Had he not stopped, he could have dragged me on the ground and only God alone could have pulled me out of disastrous results. I was not much of a religious person, but this event brought me to pray and believe that my guardian angel saved me from total destruction. That grueling experience induced me to decide that teaching was not my calling.

◆ ◆ ◆

My Civil Service eligibility was the key that opened my employment in city government in 1925. I landed a job in the Land Tax Division and Internal Revenue Section, Municipal Treasurer's Office. One of my co-workers was a co-graduate in high school. Working together, we became very close friends and allies. Between the two of us, we connived, contrived, and planned to seek our fortune and destiny abroad. Hawaii was our initial intended destination, but fate and financial considerations[11] brought us to America, the land of the free.

I was a steerage passenger amongst 29 Filipinos on the SS President Cleveland which sailed from Manila bound for Seattle, Washington. Stopovers included Hong Kong, Shanghai, Kobe, and Yokohama.

The steerage, our living quarters, was dirty, with the stench of rotten garbage. Our food, prepared and served by Chinese "coolies," was for the hogs. What rations we were supposed to have were denied us, then sold back to us by these Chinese. Fruit, oranges, and apples in our rations ended up in their possession and were sold back to us at exorbitant prices. In the end, we wound up grabbing them without paying. One day during the trip, after leaving Japan, we were served the worst food imaginable. Us *pinoys* together agreed to do something about it. We dumped the food in a tray and decided to bring it to the attention of the captain of the ship. A Visayan and I were chosen to carry out the plan. We didn't succeed in reaching the captain, but other officers thankfully heard our legitimate complaints, and the quality of our meal considerably improved. Fruit was served freely and the trip became more bearable.

While in Yokohama, I had the pleasure of meeting the famous and exiled General Ricarte[12]. Robust and healthy, he inspired me not to forget our country and to love the Philippines forever as he has done. His sincerity and his desire to go back to the homeland, when and if allowed, rang a patriotic inspiration on me, which was etched indelibly in my mind for many years.

I landed in Seattle, Washington, in April of 1926,[13] not knowing a single person, and with only five dollars in my pocket.

2. MY MILITARY EXPERIENCE

My father never did talk much about his military days, and I don't think it was something that ever defined him. But he was extremely patriotic, both to his native Philippines and to America. I do know that he was quite proud of his service through the American Legion, which he proudly served for many decades.

> "Ask not what your country can do for you; ask what you can do for your country."
>
> —PRESIDENT JOHN F. KENNEDY

Prior to World War II, Filipinos residing in mainland USA, were unwanted nationals not eligible to become American citizens. We were no better than third-class residents, absolutely denied all the rights, privileges, and conveniences enjoyed by other residents and citizens. There were always "no rooms in the inn" for us, save for the ghettos and oriental districts, the Chinatowns or Japan towns, in America. We could not purchase nor lease real property. We could not legally marry Caucasian women, though in some cases we were permitted to live with them in sin. We were denied services in most eating establishments. Although permitted to enroll in schools, we were segregated and ignored. The only jobs available regardless of education were stoop labor, janitors, or dishwashers. If we wanted to attend a movie house or theater, a certain designated area was our only choice. If we dared to tread on public streets, there would be heard insulting remarks, such as "gogos" or "monkeys." We could not even freely commune with our Creator within the walls of churches or synagogues.

And then came December 8, 1942.

The surprise attack by the Japanese Imperial Army on the Philippines catapulted the nationalism and love of country by Filipinos everywhere in mainland USA. Although their problems and plights were ignored by both Philippine officials and the Philippine government previous to that infamous day, Filipinos residing in America congregated, schemed, and plotted to redeem the glory of their home country.

In Salinas, where we had a working, organized community, nightly sessions were assembled to discuss the ways and means to prove our heartfelt love of country. Torrid debates on *how to save the country* were the central theme of these discussions.

"You are traitors!" shouted those favoring armed action.

"You are angry zealots who understand not the implications of your positions!," retorted others who felt the government should do the planning and directing. We surely were divided; we waited, however, to await planned action by the powers that be. And it came swiftly. With almost united agreement between the Philippine Government and the United States, the induction of Filipino US residents into the US Armed Forces became a reality. In spite of all the indignities suffered by these Filipino nationals, they were inducted into all branches of the Armed Forces.

We were directed to fight to preserve the freedom that was denied us; for liberty we never enjoyed and for a country that failed to protect us. I have been reliably informed by a knowledgeable legal advocate that as nationals not eligible for American citizenship, inducting us into the Armed Forces was an illegal action of the US government. But without protest, we became men of war.[14]

I was one of the many who was selected to train to defend liberty, freedom and democracy. (Birthday present...June 17, 1942...from Washington, DC...You are in the Army now.) When the war started, I was being treated for an enlarged heart, but at the induction center, my examining "doc" didn't even bother to render me the routine test. He scribbled his John Doe on my enlistment, so I could only say, "Sir, I am ready to serve."

I was classified and assigned to join contingents of Filipinos at San Luis Obispo Army Camp, but after our numbers increased, we became the First and Second Infantry Regiments,[15] constituted and trained in Salinas, California. We were segregated, interned, and then housed in the same buildings vacated by the Japanese internees of World War II. The barracks were dilapidated wooden structures with insufficient facilities, including no hot water in the communal showers. The situation of these trainees fighting for freedom and democracy seemed no better than the living conditions of the Japanese prisoners whose only crime was they were Japanese.

As our numbers multiplied—recruits came from all sections of the United States—the Interment Center became inadequate for our numbers. We were first moved to Fort Ord; later the First Regiment was shipped to Camp Beale, California, and the Second Regiment to Lompoc, California. Hunter Liggett Reservation and Camp Roberts were arenas for training and maneuvering purposes.

My stint as a "civilian soldier" was a series of disappointments. First, at the induction center, the classification officer indicated without reservation that I should best be assigned to an Air Force Brigade. This was after a deliberate analysis of my papers, which he amazingly shared with the other classifying personnel following his tail. I learned later that his deduction was strictly based on the results of IQ and mechanical aptitude tests. These tests were given to all draftees. I was classified and assigned to the Filipino Regiment, nonetheless.

My personal dissatisfaction of Army life commenced when, because of inadequate medical instruments and supplies, treatment of my enlarged heart was temporarily discontinued. For weeks, I was kept confined alone in the barracks while my comrades were close order drilling in the surrounding terrain. I was not missing any training, however, for basic training was old hat to me. Remember my ROTC training in high school! I finally forced myself to join the training.

While yet at the interment compound, my disappointment was incensed by the personal order of a shavetail of a lieutenant that forced the entire company in formation to attend Sunday Catholic masses. Now, I was baptized into the Philippine Independent Church, the Aglipayan Church. We were Catholics who had separated from Roman or Spanish Catholicism, so we ignored the Latin rites and used local vernacular instead. The Aglipayan Church also allowed priests to marry, and we refused to pay unjust taxes to the Vatican. Being non-Catholic,[16] I rebelled against his orders. And my resistance surely did not satisfy his ego. We never did see eye-to-eye again. The inexperienced headquarters personnel also misplaced my so-called service records, another factor of distrust between me and my superior officers. For the duration of five months, it was routine for the troops to stand in long lines to receive their meager pittance: $21/month, then $50/month for privates. When I reached the table of the paymaster, I was dejectedly informed that I was not on the payroll. No dinero for personal necessities.

My superiors, for five months, promised to have this problem resolved, yet nothing happened. I managed to get a day pass after five pay days of frustration and managed to get a partial pay from headquarters. My success enraged all my superiors, from the First Sergeant to the Company Commander, as they accused me of going over their heads. In my mind, I only succeeded to accomplish in a day what they failed to do in five months.

◆ ◆ ◆

There was a pressing need for commissioned officers. After learning that I was adequately qualified for Officer Candidate School, I filled my application for consideration. My friends went to OCS and came back as commissioned officers, but I was never informed as to the consequence of my application. One weekend, however, I was on duty as CQ (Charge of Quarters). I found my OCS application hidden in the office files. My superiors never had the intention of submitting the papers to the proper channels, a retaliation perhaps to questions I asked that puzzled them considerably. My relationship with my superiors deteriorated tremendously. Then the inevitable happened.

I had a verbal and physical confrontation with my First Sergeant, an Anglo, who loved to indulge heavily on liquor. One evening, I left the compound with the proper pass showing that I was free from 6:00 p.m. At retreat at 6:30 p.m., I was reported absent. The next morning before formation, I was summoned to report at the Company office. The First Sergeant angrily berated me for being AWOL. I responded by presenting him with a legal pass which bore the genuine signature of the Commanding Officer. It angered him more when I accused him of not being able to read and comprehend what he was reading. He threatened me that I would be demoted, and he surely was manly cursing.[17] I bluntly told him that he scared me not and if he accepted my challenge, I would fight him in front of the company which was then proceeding morning formation. He lunged at me; I dodged and smacked him in the face. He staggered and fell to the floor.

We could have continued our struggle if not for the intervention of all the company officers, who were at the adjoining room listening to all that was happening. I was not betrayed by the officers and luckily given any form or punishment, save maybe that I never was given a three-day pass. Once I requested three-days leave and my superior refused my request declaring, "If I grant your wish, who would be in charge of your squad?" I retorted without hesitation that I had a man (he had two years of college) who could take over; he knew more than any of your beloved sergeants. Request was again denied, indeed!

Our battalion was tenting and maneuvering at Hunter Liggett Reservation when I received a surprise order. Without my superior's awareness, I had orders to report to headquarters, Camp Roberts, for new assignments. This was during evening mess; I packed my gear and left my company wondering why and what was my fate. There were a number of us who were sent to different assignments and destinations. I was directed to report to Ohio State University in Columbus, Ohio.

We left Camp Roberts after an early light breakfast and arrived at the Oakland Terminal very famished at about 4:00 p.m., scheduled to take the train an hour later. To satisfy our hunger, three of us scrambled to a diner within proximity of the station. Initially, we were refused admittance, then permitted to enter. We sat down at the stalls and the server demanded that we pay in advance for our meals. Finally, another employee approached us and practically threw us out of the establishment. Hungry and boiling mad at such undignified treatment, I decided to make it an issue and start a confrontation. I strongly believed that it was more of an affront to the uniform of an American soldier, than to the honor of a Filipino. My companions, both shy and meek, who never had rebelled even for a just cause, pleaded with me to calm down, and ignore the whole incident. We settled for lunch boxes which we devoured in our train compartments. However, my blood continued to rise when we could account for $2,000 in our possession and we were insulted by being ordered to pay in advance for $2.50 meals.

Another interesting experience I encountered during my months in the Filipino Regiments was the ultimate cancellation of my proposed assignment to the Counter-Intelligence Corps. I was recommended, interviewed, and later qualified to join the force, although I never applied for this assignment. However, strict personal backgrounds were carefully conducted by the FBI for this assignment.[18] A soldier was also deliberately planted in my company to watch me. The company personnel never knew of his mission. After several weeks in our company with seemingly friendly relations with me, he disappeared, and we believed he went AWOL.

Finally, I was turned down by the CIC, but not because of

an unfavorable report by the disappearing soldier. They had uncovered evidence of past activities as a "militant" labor leader.[19] Although I was cleared by the Salinas Court of Law from accusations as a radical, troublemaker, communist, etc., the FBI found records in Monterey County and in the US Government Civil Liberties Investigating Committee branding me as such. The false records prevailed, and the court decision was ignored.[20]

We were stationed at the Ohio State University Stadium Dormitory for tests and evaluations, then scattered and assigned to various north eastern universities for prescribed studies. We were told in no uncertain terms that these studies should last six months—no more—and then we would be commissioned as officers in the US Armed Forces. Because of my high test scores, I was chosen to report to Yale University via Camp Sterling in Saint Paul, Minnesota. The program we joined was the Army Specialized Training Program.[21] I was to learn Nihongo (Japanese) and train as a military administrator. The course was extensive and comprehensive to some of the student soldiers, mostly privates and PFCs and a few commissioned officers. The course appeared a breeze. Most of the students were professional businessmen, few were not college graduates. There were more than several PhDs. Most could without difficulty be inducted into MENSA. And I was the only mere stoop laborer. The six months or instruction was extended to almost a year, the courses of studies stopped, but the promise or a commission was denied to us. Our only consolation was the assurance by Pentagon brass that our qualifications were far superior to the ninety-day wonders, those Army officers who exceeded numerically the table of Army organizations. While at Yale, we sported the insignia of the Third Air Force.

The course of studies was strenuous and comprehensive. Neither were we exempt from regular Army soldier's duties and training. We had several lecturers on the life, histories, customs, and traditions of the Japanese, Chinese, Micronesians, Indonesians, and Pacific Islanders. Weekly reading assignments—about a hundred pages per lecturer—were added to the lectures and army duties. Books for extra reading assignments were so few compared to the number of soldiers reading them. The language I was required to learn was Japanese, while others learned Chinese, and still others Pacific and Oriental vernaculars.

One of our lecturers on Japanese was a journalist who was caught living in Japan at the start of the Pacific War. How he escaped from Japan was never revealed. On one of his lectures, he belittled the raid by the Doolittle Squadron, saying that the damage inflicted by the raid was meaningless and insignificant, and that a bonfire during any US college homecoming was bigger and more damaging. This statement stirred plenty of uproar and the local papers disputed his declarations. People were taken by surprise; they had been previously informed by the press and media of the devastating effects of the gallant, surprise attack.[22]

While at Yale, word was loosely spreading that there was a need for volunteers for overseas duties—probably frontline positions were needed. Some, including myself, tired and disgusted by the strenuous program, filed applications. But nary any soul was tapped for the war front assignment. Then came the information that the Filipino Infantry Regiments were going overseas. I pleaded with the powers that be to release me from ASTP so I could rejoin my old company. I was advised (and found later dumbly unreliable) that the only alternative to pursue a release was to flunk my study courses. I deliberately followed this advice. I found to my chagrin that instead of being released, I was severely punished. My cherished Class A pass was confiscated from my possession, and I was ordered to utilize my whole efforts toward my studies until my grades improved.

You can't actually win in the Army. Just obey orders. Dead or Alive!

◆ ◆ ◆

Before we bury the Yale University episode, may I reveal an incident that gave me a big kick. While I was a GI student, the New York City Office of Information, which regularly broadcasted to the Philippines, ordered me to report at their center. They directed me to tape messages of encouragement to the people of the Philippines to be transmitted repeatedly to that devastated nation. However, for safety reasons, my identity was not openly revealed for protection of those bearing my name. My voice—and my uplifted spirits—reached the Philippines. And so, my family may have heard me. I was able to visit my homeland in voice, but my body never tread the *Pearl of the Orient Seas*.[23]

◆ ◆ ◆

The dreaded Yale University experience was followed by an assignment at McDill Air Force Base (4th Air Force) at Tampa, Florida, a place teaming with commissioned officers, sprinkled with a handful of enlisted men. Our contingent, coming fresh from ASTP, swelled the ranks of the lowly GI. But we were not wholeheartedly welcomed. When and where we came from became evident. We were jealously dubbed "The Whiz Kids," of which connotation we chose to ignore.

My training as an infantry soldier with the Filipino Regiments, specifically as a squad leader on the machine gun and mortar sections, was a great asset which made my assignment at this air base a breeze. Very few soldiers, including the commissioned officers, had this background. Twenty- or twenty-five-mile hikes were scheduled. It was optional for me to be with the troops. I usually walked with them, nonetheless. During lectures on the nomenclature or performance of the M1 Rifle or the 20-mm or 30-mm machine guns, I was allowed to leisurely spend my time apart from the rest of the men. My service record already manifested my successful completion of these special trainings. Just once during our training, the sergeant asked me, not ordered me, to demonstrate to the troops my comprehension of these tools of destruction. I dismantled them, explaining the detailed functions of the parts, then reconstructed them without any pressing problems. In the infantry, these processes were made part of your life; I used to do them blind-folded or on dark nights without difficulty. There were times, however, that my services were taxed to my dismay. There were times when curiosity got the best of some young GIs and against regulations, they would dismantle the trigger assembly of the rifle. Instead of bringing the disassembled irons to the armorer or other trained personnel, it was more convenient for them to have me solve the dilemma.

There was one day that the troops were scheduled to go on bivouac. I was thinking that we would go to some wilderness away from civilization, but my expectations turned out to be a laughing experience. Where do you think we went? Not out yonder, not in the secluded, untamed terrain, but into the open wide spaces of the camp parade grounds. We, in full military gear, were herded into the field, scattered throughout the perimeter, to lazily idle our time. The brass were in conferences, obviously not prepared for the program at hand or for the lowly GIs wondering what our objective were. Recall that the commissioned officers were ninety-day wonders, and it became apparent that they were not particularly knowledgeable about the assigned task.

After some inquiring, I learned that we were to pitch tents and rough it out overnight. I decided to go ahead and pitch my tent so that I could rest my head comfortably. A young private close and friendly to me for some reason managed to be by my side. I directed him to unpack his half of the pup tent while I took out mine and in the twinkling of an eye, both of us were luxuriating within the confines of our shelter. My leisure did not last forever, to my disgust. I was then ordered to instruct and supervise the building of a tent city. Such was the great American, know-it-all, US Army.

◆ ◆ ◆

Some members of our ASTP group, especially the many

multi-language experts, graduates from European universities, and those who fluently spoke and understood European languages, were retained at McDill AFB and assigned to become voice interceptors, translators and/or interpreters. Others, including me, were reassigned to an isolated secret Army Training Base at Warrenton, Virginia, not far from Arlington and Washington, D.C. We were informed that originally, we would be billeted in parts of the town with per diems and be transported to and from the hidden base for instructions. This plan was cancelled, however, when it became evident that there were barracks at the camp.

The travel from McDill to Warrenton was the worst I experienced in my many ordered travels in the US Armed Forces. We travelled overnight in soot-infested cattle cars. So when we arrived at our destination the next morning, we discovered an absurd phenomena—all of us were all of the same color. Skin wise, we were totally coal-soot blacks. We, however, just laughed at the experience.

There were two courses of specialized instruction at the camp: Traffic Analysis and Crypto-Analysis. My assignment was the latter. This camp was not listed openly to the public. It was built under towering trees, so that a plane flying above could not identify the barracks. It was also circled and protected by barbed wire and guarded by fully armed sentinels. All students were strictly informed not to mention the camp by name to outsiders, even to other soldiers not affiliated to the camp. We were instructed not to identify our location, but to mention some other bases within the proximity of Washington. If on leave to town, I spent most of my time-offs in the nation's capital.

Classes were strictly monitored. We were bodily searched after daily instructions, and any piece of paper found in your possession was confiscated and burned by armed guards. Crypto-analysis, my assigned course of study—a very challenging subject—proved to me a surprisingly enjoyable course of study. A week or so prior to the completion of the course, an order from higher-ups arrived, and all foreign-born personnel in the program were unceremoniously detached and shipped to other installations. There were never clear explanations to justify the abrupt action. The fact that we were not native Americans was apparent before assignment. The knowledge I learned, even if they didn't graduate me and didn't award me the promised laurels after the completion of study, could not be extracted from me. At the next assignment, believe it or not, I was at times prevailed upon to put my knowledge to use. Well, the great American democracy and its prestigious Armed Forces works undeterred in many wasteful and mysterious ways.

Though I was assigned different locales, I sported the insignia of the 4th Air Force up to my discharge.

Pinedale, a Signal Corps installation in the grape-growing central California, was my next destination. Part of my assignment surprisingly involved the use of the instructions at the Crypto-Analysis School where I was recently barred. I worked side-by-side with Japanese-Hawaiian *neseis*, listening and taping Japanese broadcasts, especially those by the infamous Tokyo Rose, and then transcribing them into clear American text. At Pinedale, I also look instruction which I completed in message center operations and management.

Most personnel at Camp Pinedale, in addition to my comrades at McDill Air Force Base and Warrenton, were earmarked for shipment to the Philippines. Being the only Filipino in the outfit, I was commissioned to instruct them in Philippine geography and basic Tagalog, the primary Philippine language. I protested and told them in no uncertain terms that my knowledge and comprehension of the Tagalog dialect[24] was so limited and inadequately lacking to give instructions. My pleas fell, nevertheless, on deaf ears. When the Army gives you an order, do it or else! With the help of an English/Tagalog dictionary which I was able to make available and some Tagalog-speaking acquaintances, I was able to compile a booklet copying the same format as was utilized in the other language booklets.

The preparations for movement into overseas assignments proceeded smoothly. Came O-Day for the detachment, and overseas gear was issued to all personnel, including myself. However, at the last moment, I received orders to unpack my gear, and the detachment was to leave without me. Undaunted by the order, I visited headquarters to protest what I believed was a blunt discrimination. Facing the Commanding Officer and his staff, I pleaded to join my outfit overseas. I reminded them that I was the only Filipino in the company. I knew and understood Filipino ways and languages, that I knew Philippine geography well and as a trained infantry soldier, no one else in the company had or received this training. At least they gave me a chance to air my position. After intently listening to my discourse, the Chief-of-Staff looked me in the eye, then calmly replied, "Soldier, we admit without reservation that you possess those family advantages, and we would love to have you with us. Your compadres will also miss you, no doubt. But it's your safety and the people of your homeland that concerns us. As you know, we are a detachment handling and possessing top secret war materials. Suppose we were in crisis, and you were taken prisoner by the enemy. Do you believe that anyone who bore your name would be spared? Think about it, soldier."

I remained in the mainland doing my best to perform my assignments.

A few weeks after my mobile outfit left for overseas assignments, I received an order to report to University of Michigan in Ann Arbor, Michigan, for additional comprehensive studies about Japan, its people, and its intricate language. These were extensions of the knowledge I acquired at Yale University. The course of study included, we were informed, preparations for secret landings on Japan soil prior to the actual invasion by the Armed Forces. Fortunately for us, the Japanese Imperial

Armed Forces surrendered unexpectedly. The fear of the secret landings disappeared, but the plan of sending us to mainland Japan did not. Instructions continued, and those who elected to remain in their soldiering for a term of not less than two years were to be shipped to Japan as officers in the Military Intelligence Corps. They were to be billeted in the prestigious and luxurious hotels of Tokyo or Yokohama.

To me and others, remembering all the broken promises of the war machine brass, the dissolutions and the pitfalls, the humiliations we suffered and experienced, made it easy to reject these future promises. We bluntly told our interviewers, "Give us the choice between being an Army major or a civilian, and we, without regrets, would prefer the freedom from Army ties."

I was discharged in September 1945 on earned points;[25] I succeeded in influencing our company clerk to add into my records the existence of family dependents (points were based on length of service plus dependents). That was the culmination of my military involvement. The Army Military Intelligence Service gave me an education, made my life easier temporarily by living in luxurious student dormitories, helped me see the country, and made me a believer that the pen is indeed mightier than the sword.[26] For after detachment from the infantry, I never had the occasion to carry a rifle much less fire one.

When someone asks me now what I did during the war, I simply smile and fondly declare that I was a “USO commando.”

3. LABOR INVOLVEMENT

My father was among the first generation (sometimes called the "Manong generation") of Filipinos to immigrate to the United States at the beginning of the twentieth century. At that time, immigration was allowed due to a lack of workers in the US, primarily farm labor and cannery workers. From Seattle to San Francisco to Los Angeles to Chicago, Pinoys trekked to this foreign land in search of the American dream.

Understand that this was a different time for the Filipino, and the nature and type of bigotry and injustice that they experienced was unique in the history of America. For example, interracial marriage was illegal (due to the Anti-Miscegenation law of 1905) and interracial dating would be at the extreme risk of beatings or lynchings. But there were also very few Filipinas available to date either. Filipinos, even highly educated ones, were socially relegated as either laborers or house boys, and it was common to set wages for Filipinos below that of other ethnic groups. Due to the migratory nature of work, there were few "Manilatowns" where culture could be celebrated and safe community could occur. And of course, Filipinos were also subjected to the same indignities of being prohibited from using restaurants, drinking fountains, restrooms, and other amenities, just like African-Americans of that time.

Things were exacerbated by the Dust Bowl migration (see note 25), where race riots became a regular occurrence, and it was dangerous to just be a Filipino. These conditions changed at the onset of World War II, when the US government, needing fighting men, offered citizenship to all Filipinos who enlisted. The Tydings-McDuffie Act of 1934, which restricted Filipino immigration to 50 people per year, was also repealed after the war. This opened the door for Filipinos to begin bringing their families and friends to the US. As you read through this next chapter, you will get a sense that my father was in the eye of the storm in all these historical events.

I, an ambitious young man, very hungry for better and higher education, managed to enroll, tuition free, as a student at the University of Idaho in Moscow, Idaho. I was attempting to become an electrical engineer, a profession which was badly needed in my beloved Philippines. This worthwhile desire was abruptly curtailed by the Great Depression of 1929, which engulfed the whole nation, if not the entire world. Wall Street crushed, rich people became bankrupt, businesses failed, the poor became poorer. It was a maddening blow to the citizenry—jobs became scarce, savings and investments disappeared, life appeared hopeless. As for me, schooling was delayed, and no jobs were available.

I moved to California in search of work. The only jobs available, however intermittently, were farm work. To survive, I plunged into stoop labor, and became a migrant peon following the crops all over California, Arizona, and even to the snowclad farms of Montana. I lived in pitched tents or grass huts or just under pine trees in the Imperial Valley, California. In Arizona, I lived in dilapidated shelters and crowded barns. I worked in crowded farms, where people were fighting to work for fifteen cents per hour and no guarantee of time work. There appeared, on occasions, that there were more workers than "carrots to be bunched." These disgraceful living conditions and the meager renumerations encouraged and inspired me to seek agreeable solutions to this shameful state of affairs.

I learned and heard about the "race riots" in El Centro, California and also in Watsonville, California. Labor camps and residences of Filipinos were raided and bombed, hurting innocent people. Fermin Tobera, a laborer and peace-loving Filipino, was killed by a bomb deliberately thrown into his living quarters while sleeping. The perpetrators of this inhumane bombing were never apprehended, nor was there concentrated any effort to find them. During these dark decades, Filipinos were endlessly blamed for lowering wages and taking away jobs from the Anglos, nay, the citizens. The gospel truth, however, was that those charges were unfounded.

The "Filipino boys," as we were grudgingly called, were merely trying to make a living in jobs the accusers never wanted to perform anyway. And the Filipinos were trying to make a living without trying to bother any person or persons. It was a situation where if you don't work, you don't eat. To survive, we had to accept any job that was available. The farmers, the growers, and the shippers knew that Filipinos were hardworking, and didn't require excessive supervision.

My experiences in agricultural farms and ranches, coupled with my better knowledge of the English language and the great trust my co-workers bestowed upon me, led me to becoming a straw boss, a labor-camp operator, during early 1930-1931.[27] I was overseeing some hundred Filipinos in the harvesting of grapes and peaches in the Reedley-Dinuba area of California, when one afternoon, the camp we were living in—a large, two-story barn situated on a crossroads with grape vineyards behind us—was surrounded by cars, trucks, and all makes of vehicles loaded with angry, threatening people. All alighted from their vehicles and entered the premises shouting and demanding to see the leader. I confronted the angry group. They demanded and ordered us to pack whatever possessions we had and not only vacate the premises within 24 hours but also to leave town. This order was accompanied by the shouts of "or else." The "or else" was a disastrous threat. That night two other Filipino labor camps were bombed. Luckily, however, no one suffered bodily harm.

The proprietor of the premises, a farmer of Armenian extraction whose parents lived through the same conditions, also owned and managed a gas station at the comer adjacent to the camp. He witnessed the threatening actions of the mob and heard their threats and ultimatums. Without hesitation, he contacted the local officials. Luckily for us, the local authorities were sympathetic to our cause. The County Sheriff Department and the Highway Patrol were contacted, and they furnished us with the necessary protection by periodically patrolling the roads leading to our camp. It was also proposed by the local authorities to set up the camp as a pseudo-military installation—and I acted explicitly.

After the mob left the premises, I told the men that if they chose to move out, they were free to go. Paychecks would be ready if they were ready. Nary a soul left. The crew stuck together, sink or swim. With the help of three members of the crew, ex-soldiers from the Philippine Scouts, the strategic plan of defense was set into motion. For many weeks until the harvest season, we had armed guards patrolling at night with orders not to hesitate to shoot any violators of our safety and privacy. The two-barrel shotguns we used for rabbit hunting served handily as our defensive weapons. The regular nightly patrolling by the local law enforcement agencies may have scared the mobs, for we never saw or heard from them again. It was also recommended that for self-protection, I carry a concealed weapon as I travelled around to check the work crews deployed in the vineyards around the territory. I declined that suggestion, however, believing that that may be a more destructive than constructive option.

After the harvest was completed, we again moved to places where there was work. Most of us went to the Imperial Valley to work the cantaloupe, carrot, and lettuce farms. We were true-to-form migrant workers, following the crop.

At that time, there were plenty of farm laborers who could hardly read or write, even in their own language. Upon the request of some of my coworkers, I would read to them messages and letters from loved ones from home and would write responses for them. With the assistance of a companion, a former school teacher in the homeland, we tutored these unfortunates to read and to write. Proudly we hailed the success of this endeavor. Many, thankful of our help, never again bothered us to read and write letters to and from loved ones. I can also attest that we were able to successfully improve the math understanding of others in our camp.

These degrading experiences prompted me to dream of a movement to help improve the living and wage conditions of the farm workers, the poverty-laden Filipino farm workers.

In the early part of 1932, I learned through the grapevine of a brewing labor uprising in the Salinas Valley in central California. I had learned from other migrant workers in the Imperial Valley that Salinas was a place where the sun spends the winters.

My small crew was engaged in the harvest of carrots in the Santa Maria-Lompoc territory, a couple of hours drive to Salinas. Curiosity prompted me to take temporary leave from my crew. I proceeded to Salinas with the primary purpose or observing, seeing first-hand the labor movement in action.

This labor exercise was supposedly a joint undertaking by the mostly Anglo cannery shed workers and the exclusively Filipino farm workers. The Filipinos harvested the crops, then transported them to the packing sheds—the Anglo domain—for packaging and distribution for the market. I entered the picture as an "observer," but I ended up joining the leadership. I became a trusted leader of the Filipino farm labor supplier, who instigated and financed the Filipino side of the struggle.

As I came to understand the situation, I saw that the movement was actually an open war between the shed and farm workers and the growers/shippers and the local leaders and law enforcement agencies, their vigilantes. The shed workers were not endeared by the local citizenry. They comprised heavily of those driven by the big drought of Oklahoma and Arkansas who settled in the eastside of Salinas, across the railroad tracks. Hence, their settlements were commonly, if not derisively, dubbed "Okie Towns."

During the movement, crops of unaccountable value were destroyed and many striker's heads, including mine, were dented by baseball clubs. The Canete Labor Camp, the foremost known financier of the Filipino faction, and his residence were pock-marked by bullets, and later burned to the ground. Firefighters were barred from extinguishing the conflagration. Nobody was ever apprehended amongst the perpetrators of the arson. Luckily, no human being was hurt at this incident. Later rumors were rampant that Filipinos themselves were the arsonic culprits—a shameful accusation indeed!!

Up to the present, I am still under a cloud as to the actual and real reason of the misunderstanding that flared between the Filipino farm workers and the Anglo shed workers. The shed union workers received recognition, but the Filipinos got the black ball. The recognition gave them the vehicle to negotiate for higher wages and better working atmosphere. The "Filipino boys," the hands that toiled the hardest, remained under the thumbs of the farmers/growers/shippers, through the unrestricted stooges, the Filipino farm labor suppliers.

The number one undermining problem of the Filipino farm workers was the preponderant lack of opportunities to engage in other remunerative endeavors, as well as the lack of places to live if they fled from the filthy, crowded labor camps. No other alternatives existed but to submit to the indignity of stoop labor—conditions paralleling, if not worse, the unsanitary situations of the cardboard shacks of illegal immigrants of today.

My experiences in the 1932 Labor Strike placed me within the roles of people interested in the welfare of the oppressed agricultural workers. In the concentrated efforts to organize and unite this group of workers into the UCAPAWA,[28] I was approached to join in the struggle. The foremost labor leader participating in the struggle was no other than the chief architect of the International Longshoremen's Union. The UCAPAWA had the total backing of the AFL.[29] However, this movement didn't fare well as a united front. We became fragmented and the groups were absorbed by various American Federation Unions.

Over time, the labor movement became a part of my dream—it became an obsession. I could no longer go back to my working crews, and I was essentially black-balled by the agricultural industry. Through it all, I continuously endeavored to preach the advantages of oneness and the necessity of unionism.

In 1936, a big push to organize and strengthen the Shed Workers and Farm Workers Unionization became a priority of the AFL. Militant Anglo labor organizers were dispatched to the Salinas Valley, and I was recruited to handle the farm workers. I was informed that Filipino leaders, nay even Filipino newspaper men, tried to get this assignment as a union organizer. Their ambitions were of course denied, for their obvious intentions were self-propelled. They possessed not the background nor the sincerity; it became obvious that their main consideration was the dinero involved. In contrast, the labor organizers were convinced of my deep-seated desire to improve the wages and living conditions of the forgotten *Pinoys*.

I set up shop in Salinas in cooperation with the Anglo organizers. When the time was ripe to move, the shed workers openly and unanimously declared a strike. We Filipinos then joined the struggle. Picket lines were positioned and roving strikers ringed the farms where scabs were working. On the other side of the coin were the farmers backed by business people, government employees with goons, the strike breakers, and the vigilantes, including local and state peace officers. Those caught within the labor camps were then detained and kept in as "prisoners." Some camps were enclosed by barbed wire fences guarded by armed sentinels. Those scabs harvesting the crops were guarded by armed, hired thugs or vigilantes. Truckers who transported the harvest were accompanied by "shotgun" accomplices. Filipino farm workers lost whatever freedom they had, and the Filipino labor bosses never protested against these indignities. Indeed, the truth was that they cherished this treatment. The strikers, on the other hand, did whatever was necessary to stop shipments. Truckers suffered flat tires, nails were strewn under trucks, windows were broken by missiles-rocks. In many instances, loaded trucks were stopped and produce was strewn on the roads and highways. No labor strike to my knowledge can top the Salinas Valley Labor Strike of 1936.[30] Gun emplacements were set up at the top of the Jeffery Hotel, the highest or tallest structure in the Valley at that time, and tear gas was freely fired in their attempts to disperse strikers.

There have been farm laborer's strikes in California but not as violent as the Salinas Valley Labor Strike of 1936. A veteran newspaperman, who was kicked out of The Salinas Californian newspaper for printing labor news factually and who personally witnessed these labor strikes said, "The labor strikes instituted by the United Farm Workers under Generalissimo

Cesar Chavez, were church socials compared to the 1936 confrontation."[31]

During the height of the strike, Chris Mensalves, a seasoned and veteran labor union organizer and leader in the Santa Maria/Lompoc areas, came to Salinas to meet me and help me strengthen and coordinate our forces. We were conducting a night meeting at the Moose Hall in Salinas when we were served with subpoenas. The charge was vagrancy. The sad part of the arrest was that a Filipino—a self-appointed, self-serving labor boss—charged us with the false accusation.

We were unjustly arrested and hauled to the Monterey County Jail, fingerprinted, mugged, and incarcerated. The AFL was promptly notified of our arrest. The best AFL legal defender was immediately dispatched to Salinas. He worked for our release and within 18 hours, we were out of the dungeon. Up to the present, I never learned who put up the property bail for our release. From the jail, we were rushed to the strike headquarters, hailed as heroes, and lavishly praised for our assistance to their cause.

Weeks after we were released and the labor strike was settled, we were ordered to appear in a court of law to answer the charges. The AFL lawyer who worked for our release defended us. He succeeded in asking and motioning the court to give Chris Mensalves and I separate trials. Through the course of the trial, the prosecutors never referred to the charge of vagrancy. It was clearly evident that prosecution intended to brand us as Communists, radicals, agitators and troublemakers. At that time, this strategy was prevalent to undermine and break up trade unions. The defense, however, vigorously argued and proved that we were and far away not what the prosecution alleged. Mensalves was unconditionally absolved from all charges. The case against me was promptly dropped.

Although the demeaning charges against me were dropped and the court declared me innocent, it was obvious that the government records still continued to perpetuate this very false accusation.[32] A Senate Civil Liberties Investigating Committee descended into Monterey a year or so after the strike, and in their records was a notation of our arrest. Monterey County records no doubt was the source of the degradation. Chris Mensalves and Manuel Luz—branded radicals, agitators, communists, troublemakers—the decision by the court was disregarded but the false accusations remained. These false accusations followed me into my Army experiences, to my great detriment.

For many seasons, I remained an active force in the Alaska Cannery Workers Union in Portland, Oregon, but I never actively participated in the organization of labor unions again. The contingent of Filipino labor leaders who assisted the Chavez' unionization efforts in the Salinas Valley in the 1960s did however seek my opinion and counsel before they stepped into green crowd territory.

When I came back to Salinas following the cessation of hostilities of World War II in 1945, I discovered that our small business, the Philippine Trading Company, a merchandising establishment, was in the down grade. It was not surprising, for many other businesses, including the downtown merchants, were duly hurt by the opening of Valley Center. Even our satellite store in Sacramento was on the losing side of the ledger. These problems were multiplied by the possibility of our landlords releasing the premises. We had to relocate to a place available, but with less traffic activity.

Looking for work became a necessary activity. Of course, I didn't want to go back to stoop-labor. So I visited the California Office Employment Department, which was then located at Monterey Street in Salinas. I was terribly shocked. It was my first ever visit to this office. When the Anglo clerk saw me close the door behind me, he came out of his cage and greeted me not with the usual, "What can I do for you?" or "Can I help you?," but with the blunt directive, "Mr. Farm Labor Boss needs men to thin lettuce. Why don't you go down and see him?" Shocking indeed.

I could not believe what I was hearing. I was insulted and stunned. Treatment like this was not the modus operandi towards other ethnic groups. Finally looking him in the eye, I stated, "If farm work is what I seek, I know better than coming to bother you here. I could go directly to any farm and work. You actually really believe that as a non-white, stoop labor is the only direction for me or for my people?"

I angrily blurted out that whites do not have a complete monopoly on education, or the ability to perform in other occupations. I was willing to bet that there were Filipinos in this vast farming area with college educations acquired from US colleges and universities. And yet, you force us to throw our education out the door when we seek employment through your facilities. I guess a furor was raised enough to bring the department manager out of his inner sanctum to mediate the question. The manager was a war veteran, a man who looked at a person as a human being, not at the color of his skin. He was understanding, courteous, and kind. He looked at my credentials and nodded his appraisal.[33] Overseas assignments were aplenty, he said, and if I so desired, he could certify my assignment to Japan without delay. I thanked him for the job offer but told him overseas duty was not my bread.

This incident was the beginning of a very good rapport between the department manager and me. We encountered each other at meetings of the American Legion. He visited Fil-Am Post 652 where I served several terms officially as Commander. And he would consult as a veteran to clarify questions relevant to the intricate workings of his department. The Salinas Office, Department of Employment, then endeavored to affect changes toward the treatment of non-Anglos.

After World War II, me and several others endeavored to establish an insurance agency in Salinas. We possessed (individually or collectively) all necessary licenses essential to operate an agency, nay even a brokerage. The partners in the LASO Insurance Agency were not functionally illiterate, ignoramuses, or stupids. Sabio was a graduate of San Jose State University;

Aquino was an alumnus of Utah State University; Olivete attended a US college and studied with the Blackstone College of Law in Chicago. Yours truly attended Idaho State University, Yale University, Michigan University and completed all the courses of studies with the Blackstone College of Law.

We contacted several insurance groups and companies and applied. A number of these companies, for courtesy sake perhaps, responded. They sent field representatives to interview us. All of these encounters ended up in irrevocable summary. To wit: "We regret to inform you that there are presently enough agencies in your area; we cannot grant any new agencies, regardless of your very commendable resumes." These rejections would not have been so hurting if we didn't have actual knowledge of new agencies, managed and owned by Anglos, who recently acquired their licenses.

We were relegated to practice our licenses by working for and under white establishments. Under the auspices of our employer, the Speegle Insurance Agency, I and the rest of my partners began to work as insurance solicitors. The LASO Insurance Agency (Luz, Aquino, Sabio, and Olivete) was born.

The color of our skin may be beautiful, but in this democratic nation, it is apparently a setback, a deterrent to a more pleasant life. We were encouraged to improve ourselves through education, but we were not given the opportunity lo practically utilize them. Is it democracy? Maybe it applied to us Filipinos if we altered the spelling to "d-e-m-o-c-r-a-z-y."

Sabio and Luz Real Estate was operating in the Salinas Valley a few years following World War II. We both successfully hurdled the required tests required by the State of California. We were legally issued our real estate broker's licenses. We even joined the Salinas multiple listing service. We put up every effort to function in accordance to the law and strictly adhere to current acceptable business practices. But our best legal efforts failed to satisfy other agencies. There were several unsubstantiated complaints filed repeatedly by our Anglo competitors to the California Real Estate Commissioner. These accusations were passed down to us. We responded to all charges to the unfailing satisfaction of the Commissioner. Once they realized their failure to substantiate their accusations, they adopted a policy of not working with us. We were never accepted in the local real estate fraternity, and we were denied partnerships with other brokers. We were lepers isolated from the body of Real Estate Brokers. Rumors also reached us that other Filipino real estate brokers were overpricing their offerings. (As if brokers set the price of real property! Brokers may suggest or advise but the real price is determined by the seller.) Fickle Filipinos relied on these rumors, however, and they shunned us. Yet, whenever they signed a contract to buy property or insurance and any misunderstanding, big or small, arose, they would come to us for. No trust in our capabilities to transact their business deals, but they had all the confidence and belief that we would successfully solve their misunderstandings without charge.

From the moment I decided to establish permanent residency in the Salinas Valley,[34] I had been sought for and engaged as an official interpreter for Filipinos by the local courts, as well as government offices and agencies. In the municipal courts, where accused Filipinos were mostly calendared, the judges themselves would personally contact me for help in most cases. Also, when problems arose concerning a Filipino, the Immigration and Naturalization Service did not hesitate to request my assistance to untangle the problem. My relationship with the Salinas INS office grew closely as I was engaged daily as an interpreter or translator.[35] I learned as they instructed me on the many phases of work and the duties of the department. Eventually, they placed so much trust and confidence in me that they allowed me—nay, encouraged me—to become an extension of their office.

My own office, a home-garage conversion, became an unofficial extension of the local INS.[36] Almost all INS forms and instructions were then made available at my home office. Nights and weekends, when the Salinas office was closed, Filipinos and Latinos used my facilities for available forms, instruction, and consultations. In most instances, I wound up filling the forms myself. Even when the Salinas office was closed by the Eisenhower administration for monetary reasons and all operations moved to the San Francisco office, residents from throughout the area knocked on my door for INS forms, assistance, and consultation. My close association with the INS opened my eyes to the gospel truth that practicing American lawyers are simply not knowledgeable to immigration. There were cases, wherein the local INS instructed me to correct or amend papers drafted by local attorneys.

I continued to offer and serve people with their immigration problems for many, many years. Looking back, it greatly elates me to realize the assistance I rendered to my people—hundreds and hundreds of Filipinos from the Philippines and Filipino *balikbayans*—for their immigration issues.[37]

The California Employment Department was another agency that required a lot of assistance from me. The manager of the establishment and I tangled on many differing views when we both served as panelists on Human Resources. One of the issues during an all-city forum sponsored by the City of Salinas was an effort to gather community input on matters affecting the city. We soon became closely allied after that confrontation. The manager persuaded me to accept a voluntary social work position as a member of the Community Action Advisory Committee.[38] One of our functions was to encourage employees and employers to patronize the facilities of the department. We, at times, were called to serve as members of panels interviewing job applicants. The department continued to avail my services when Filipinos came to the office. As a member of the committee, I saw that many other ethnic groups had their own interpreters and advocated for the employment of Filipinos in the department, preferably those who could speak *Tagalog* and/or *Ilocano*. My pleadings fell on deaf ears. I also continued to be called upon on emergencies.

Then a statewide conference of all Department of Employment managers and Advisory Committee members was urgently summoned. I was chosen and was invited to attend this pow-wow, held at a building at the San Francisco airport. Throughout the course of the conference, the subject of encouraging both employers and employees to patronize the facilities of the Department of Employment were discussed. Representatives from all over the state strongly supported this proposition. I decided then that it was a big opportunity for me to expound on a proposition which was not acceptable at my home base. After being granted time to speak, I argued that Filipinos comprised the bulk of agricultural laborers in California; that the majority of them have limited comprehension of the English language; and that the only way they could use the department facilities was to bring an interpreter.

Salinas, I declared, had been using my valuable time for occasions where Filipinos were concerned. The Latinos had Latino clerks to help them, and the Chinese had their own, so why not employ Filipino clerks to take care of their own? Not long after the conference, the local manager phoned me and cheerfully told me that a Filipina was hired and assigned at Salinas. All I said was, "Thank you! Hallelujah!"

◆ ◆ ◆

Many times when I was called upon to help a Filipino at the California Department of Employment, I invariably asked the manager to find me a job. But he doubted my sincerity. Maybe he was threatened by my demands, because one day he threw me an application for employment at the State Department of Corrections. I particularly didn't relish the prospect of working in a prison. I had no definite knowledge of the nature of the job, nor had I met any employee of the department. Neither had I read any book, papers, or pamphlets expounding the status of the profession. Curiosity more than desire ultimately prompted me to submit the application. I took all the required and necessary tests, written, oral, and physical. Surprisingly, I successfully passed all of them.

This was no small feat. I was the first Filipino to have dared seek employment in this line of work. My last interviewer, a captain, noticing perhaps my uneasiness, honestly and bluntly cautioned me, saying, "If we hire you, are you prepared to face possible discrimination? Even from among your co-workers?"

Without a minute of hesitation, I responded, "Sir, you cannot put me in a place worse than I have been before, nor discriminate against me worse than I have been discriminated before."

There was one obstacle that separated me from being hired sooner. The directives required that applicants should be at least 5 feet 8 inches in height. I was only 5 feet 4 inches. However, the captain assured me that the height requirement would be waived. And it was.

So in 1957, I became a correctional officer with the California Department of Corrections, the first Filipino in the state. A tremendous challenge was in my hands. As a pioneer, I had to serve efficiently and with respect. My personal pride was not only at stake—in a sense, it was the whole Filipino race on trial. I must have served well, for currently the Department is teeming with Filipino employees, and some of them have risen to management levels of administration.[39]

One of my first assignments at the Department was to oversee inmates working in the institution farms, where vegetables were grown for their consumption. We would then have fresh vegetables—lettuce, carrots, cabbages—direct from the farm to the kitchen. The farm manager, a veteran from the local agricultural industry, welcomed my presence. Other officers didn't have my farm labor knowledge, and soon I had improved the skills of work crews. Production multiplied, and as inmates became more adept, had more leisure time. Unfortunately, over time, the vegetable farms were dismantled because of protests by growers who missed the business of supplying the institution with fresh vegetables.[40]

Mrs. Connie Nerez was a family friend employed as a kindergarten teacher in one of the schools in Seaside, California. She was a former high-school teacher in the Philippines before coming to America. She married a correctional officer who became one, at my encouragement. Her teaching credentials were acquired by studying when her children were in high school or in college.

An incident occurred in 1954, whereby she had attained information that a forum was being conducted by the school superintendent, in conjunction with other black school administrators. But she was unable to encourage any of the Filipino leaders in the Monterey-Seaside area to attend this important meeting. Distressed by their lack of interest, Mrs. Nerez approached me, as president of the Filipino Community of Salinas Valley, Inc. (FCSV) and as Commander of Fil-Am Post 652, the American Legion.[41] My initial reaction was not to encroach on territory outside my sphere of influence. She ultimately got convinced me by reminding me that the area of membership in the FCSV included areas within 50 miles from Salinas to Monterey. Therefore, this was definitely part of my jurisdiction.

The main subject of the gathering was the planning of actions to continue an on-going program in the local schools. The program relied on finances from the federal government and sources for funding were being cut. In the program, would-be teachers were instructed and prepared for the teaching profession. Preparations consisted of half-day instruction with the other half in actual practice in the classrooms—a fine and commendable program indeed. These would-be teachers were instructed and evaluated by veteran educators and administrators. Together, Mrs. Nerez and I attended the forum.

I asked for and was granted permission to address this group of educators. I praised the excellence of the program. Then I informed the group that many Philippine-trained teachers living and working in Monterey County were performing jobs not commensurate with their education and training. I pointed out their desire to go back to their original calling if only the opportunities were available. With sincerity, I devoutly pleaded with them to include some of these "misplaced" educators in this laudable innovative program. Thankfully, they did listen to me; Unfortunately, they also did not definitely commit themselves. Also, there was no assurance that finances were available to continue the program. There was no sure answer whatsoever.

However, the next school year was a happy one indeed, for a good number of Filipinos were accepted to actively participate in the program. Several made the grade, and they were hired as classroom teachers.

Many years ago, I was invited to serve in the Administrative Committee of the Salinas Valley Memorial Hospital. I served as secretary of this committee which functioned, among other things, as overseer of the hospital's financial dealings. Over the course of time, it became apparent that the Filipina nurses employed were moving away, and although other Filipinas applied for employment—even when there was a pressing need for registered nurses—not one was hired.

A number of those who applied told me that their applications were filed, but then were told, "don't call us, we'll call you." And the hospital never contacted them again. Eventually, there remained only one registered nurse employed by the hospital.[42] Filipina nurses were pointing out that they could never be blamed for thinking that the SVMH is an institution that discriminated against Filipinos.

One night after a meeting of our administrative committee, I decided to confront the assistant administrator on this seemingly discriminatory situation. Point blank, I asked him if there was an existing hospital policy that discriminated against Filipina nurses. I updated him on the treatment by the personnel office affecting Filipina RNs applying for employment. He was genuinely shocked at my declarations. He assured me that the hospital had no policy of discrimination, and that his office had no knowledge of what the personnel office was doing. He vowed to me that he would personally order them to clean up their act. He further promised me that if an applicant was treated in the way I had described, to tell the applicant to see him personally, or for me to accompany such applicant to his office. It was quite the reassuring directive.

A mere two days after my conversation with the assistant administrator, while my family was enjoying lunch in a Chinese restaurant in town, a Filipina nurse, employed in the San Mateo area, approached us. She told me she wanted to relocate to Salinas to be near relatives and wanted to practice her training in Salinas. I suggested to her to go to Memorial Hospital and apply for a job. Moreover, she was to see the assistant administrator if need be and mention my name. She followed my advice, and she was accepted for immediate employment without question.[43]

Today, any day or night, visit the SVMH and you will see many dignified, respected Filipina nurses in immaculate whites efficiently caring for their patients. The Administrative Committee is no longer in existence. To handle bigger and more complex functions, expansions, constructions, and increasing medical programs, it was inevitably expanded from 12 members to 42 local leaders and the name was modified to Salinas Valley Memorial Hospital Foundation, Inc. It is now run by a Board of Governors.

I served in this Board for several three-year terms. This Board of Governors succeeded in raising several million dollars to enable the hospital to expand its facilities and provide new specialized technologies. During my time, SVMH became the biggest and most modem hospital between San Jose and Santa

Barbara,

During my tenure with the Board of Governors, it was my pride and joy to herald the participation of several Filipino organizations in contributing thousands of dollars for hospital expansions. The Filipino Community of Salinas Valley, the Filipino Community of Castroville, American Legion Fil-Am Post 652, the Legionarios del Trabajo, and the Fil-Am Civic League all contributed. And I am also proud to be a member of all these social-civic groups.

After leaving the Board of the SVMH Foundation, I was recruited to serve as a member of the Board of Governors of a smaller local hospital, the Salinas Community Hospital, wherein I served until it permanently closed its doors.

4: IF YOU DO NOT WORK, YOU SHALL NOT EAT

My dad was never above work. Whether it was building an extra room onto the house, or filing paperwork, or making dinner for the family, he always impressed upon us the importance of working hard and having pride in it. From Sitka, Alaska, to the Yakima Valley in Washington, to the Imperial Valley of California, and finally to our hometown in Salinas, my dad and his fellow compadres tilled the soil and planted the seed and harvested the crops. There is a quiet dignity that comes from such work, and one can wonder—does one shape the land, or does the land shape you?

It may not be your profession, but it is your avocation by necessity.

We Filipinos in the USA—regardless of profession, ability, experience, or knowledge learned in the home country or even from mainland universities and colleges—were never given the opportunity to make a living commensurate to our qualifications. Instead, Filipinos were relegated to the lowest rung of the employment picture. We did not live; we merely survived. However, we never, sought, demanded, or asked for alms. God forbid; we simply tried to live honestly through our brawn and our sweat.

I will herewith attempt to enumerate—not necessarily in chronological order—the various employments I experienced to survive in this "land of opportunity."

The first job I filled upon arriving in America in 1926 was as a "schoolboy" for a family of a university professor at the University of Washington in Seattle. The professor had two sons who were musicians on the steamship Dollar Lines, which ran between Manila and Seattle. Thus, they were a family who understood the Filipino. My chores comprised of the preparation of family meals, cleaning and clearing the sinks. On weekends,

I did general housecleaning, scrubbing the floors on all fours. I was, however, free every weekday during the day to attend school. Hence, the work moniker was "schoolboy." However, I was not enrolled in any school activity whatsoever. One very bright spot of my job which I enjoyed immensely was the open contact with the thousands of books in the household library. This library was a separate building from the house mansion, and I was responsible for keeping it clean and in proper order. After several months at this employment, I said goodbye to my kind employers to work in the lumber yards in Cosmopolis, Washington.

The box factory was my first assignment. I operated a machine shaping parts of wooden boxes and containers. From the inside, I was transferred to the company yard, where freshly sawed lumber was piled and dried. The aged lumber was then trucked to the box factory for processing. Finally, I again was moved to the real mill where the huge logs were sawed, sorted, and shipped to the open yard for aging and drying. All these movements were sort of promotions. The pay at the box factory was ten cents an hour less than at the lumber mill.

This establishment employed hundreds of laborers scattered in an area of several acres. One of the unbelievable phenomena which the new employee could not keep wondering about was the way they kept track of the working time of every employee. When you were first hired, the foreman of the division assigned you to a particular position. He never asked for your name. He was only interested in having you work and perform efficiently. Work was ten hours per day. Once in the morning and once in the afternoon, the timekeeper made his rounds lo check those who were working. If he noticed a new employee, he approached him and asked him to write his name on a piece of lumber. That would be the first and last time he would ask who you were. I never in my employment in this company heard of any employee who complained about unregistered time.

Employment in the lumber mills made me completely aware of my homesickness. The work was hard, strenuous and physical. Every night when I went to sleep, my aching body would wake me up. My fingers, sore and stiff; my hands, dotted with calluses. Every letter I tried to compose had to be written in stages. No letter was finished in one sitting. Tears, believe it or not, would fall profusely onto my writing pad to the point that if I persisted to etch my feelings, the paper would be fully tear-saturated. But when the night was over, back to the pits I went, uncomplaining.

There were happy memories related to my being a mill laborer. There were many Filipinos working here, especially in the box factory. Some of the old-timers established places for us to congregate in our spare time. We even tried to organize a Filipino Community Association, in which I attracted the personal friendship of the most recognized and settled Pinoy leader in the Cosmopolis region. He pushed me into service as one of the officers of that embryonic Filipino community.

We lived simply and thriftily in Cosmopolis. Our monthly expenses through our community sharing were the equivalent of only three days labor. We planted a vegetable garden in our backyard. The house we lived in was a stone's throw off the river, which abounded with succulent fish. After the day was done at the mill, as someone in the house prepared the rice, our staple food, someone went fishing and others would tend to the garden. Before the rice was done, the fishers would come in with the catch and the others would tend with the greens. We would then enjoy our companionship luxuriating in our home cooking.

◆ ◆ ◆

For want of further adventure and to see more of beautiful America, a couple of friends and I ventured to California, choosing San Francisco, the city of seven hills, as our destination. The year was 1927, and here I found employment in a battery factory. I was in charge of a number of pressing machines, shaping and cutting parts for dry-cell batteries. I maintained, cleaned, and was in complete charge of this department. Filipinos were trusted employees of this business concern.

San Francisco was then a cosmopolitan city, a city that welcomed Asians and permitted them to settle down. There existed, as is now, a Chinatown and a Japantown. The Filipinos, however, chose not to live in a separate barrio of their own. They were scattered, un-united, and lived in either the Chinese or Japanese settlements. Most Filipinos elected to reside in Chinatown, congregating there for amusement or just for companionship. Troubles caused by tribal differences were plentiful, so my travelling companions and I rarely visited those troublesome spots. For pleasure and amusement, we preferred the movie theaters, where aside from the movie offerings, featured stage shows with live entertainers and big bands.

Foot loose and fancy free, we decided to return to Seattle to join the exodus of Filipinos in the fish canneries of rich, beautiful, sparsely populated Alaska. The fish canneries were owned by corporations maintaining central offices in Seattle. Cannery workers were mostly recruited in Seattle, as canneries offered contracts drawn on a seasonal basis. Contracts included, aside from the monetary compensation, free round-trip transportation from Seattle to whatever cannery chosen, as well as free food and lodging. We were paid upon returning to the port of departure, however, and advanced payments were granted when essentially needed.

My first encounter with snow was when we landed at the first fish cannery I went to. The ship that brought the crew was a huge seafarer but was not high enough to give us a view of the bunk house which was to be our home for the duration of the canning season. Between the ship and the bunk house were huge mountains of glaring snow. We had to shovel to get ourselves to the bunkhouse. Shocked by the freezing white stuff, the warmth emanating from the fireplace upon our arrival was a very welcome relief.

The cannery had been closed, lock and barrel, during the winter months. We had to prepare, arrange, and settle down equipment and gear before starting the fundamental task of the canning season. The initial task was to prepare the wooden boxes, containers for shipping the marketable, delicious, canned pearls of the sea. I qualified for the crew which nailed the wooden boxes. Each nailer was allotted a quota of two hundred boxes per day. Once you met your assignment, you were free to do as you wish for the day. I became adept at box making and by 2 p.m., my quota was usually met, so I was free as a lark for the rest of the day.

But there was nowhere to go. The settlement was limited to the cannery, the warehouse, our bunk house, and the superintendent's residence and supply house. Water and more water in front, and mountains behind. Our recreations were limited to fishing, which could be done just by sitting by your window during high tide, or playing basketball till the sun set before midnight. Fish trolling was fun, playing tag with a man-sized salmon on the end of your line.

There were several positions in a fish company to wit: butchering, fish washing, running the tin can lines, canning, processing, catching cans, warehouse work, and fish sorter. In my many years working at fish canneries in different locations, I experienced and worked all of these different assignments. I not only enjoyed the work, I also enjoyed the comradeship of the coworkers.

In Sitka, Alaska, a thriving commercial and educational center, I was a member of a crew who opened the first fish cannery in that city. The crew—all single, young blades—were mostly self-supporting students from high school or college. So school colors were openly displayed, and some of us were identified by the school we attended. I myself was named "Idaho," the educational institution of my choice.

We were warmly welcomed by the residents when we arrived, and we heartily accepted their hospitality. Independence Day was celebrated, and with the sanction of the company, the cannery crew joined in the festivities. We built a float and marched in the parade to the pleasure of the populace. The local school band furnished the music. Our float was made unique and colorful by accommodating our rondel (a music group), hidden in the float's interior, which played lively tunes as the parade went on. This pleased the entire city, no doubt.

My stay in Sitka was a memorable episode in my life, but it ended in a regretful consequence, one which forced me to have to escape from Sitka unnoticed and without the approval of our contractor.

There prevailed an Alaskan regulation which was made widely known to all fish cannery crews. Whenever an Alaskan native girl became amorously involved with an alien worker, all the lady in love had to do was point out the object of her affection to any marshal in the territory, and the male, without due process, would be legally bound to live within Alaskan territory for no less than a year. However, I was quite unaware of this rule. A young RussianAlaskan lady was a regular visitor to our compound, and in all our merriments, she would always seek out "Idaho." Apparently, the entire crew was aware of the situation. Now, I never did encourage or demonstrate any amorous intentions to this young native, although I must admit she was cute, desirable, and interesting. The entire crew warned me to be cautious and watch my actions.

Eventually, the canning season ended, and those not needed as labelling and warehouse personnel were to be shipped back to Seattle. I was chosen to stay. However, when the ship arrived to pick up cargo and passengers, I, with the confidential knowledge of a fellow Idahoan, snuck onto the boat as a stowaway. The day after my unscheduled departure, I was informed that everybody was searching for me, unaware of my sudden disappearance, wondering to no end where the hell I was. The young, enamored lady had stood by the dock, saddened, crying her heart out. I never did dare accept another assignment to Sitka, although I craved the offerings of the city, which were not prevalent in other canneries I worked.

As previously mentioned, we Filipino immigrants were only welcomed to earn our livings as janitors, servants, dishwashers, and stoop-laborers. My first introduction to farm peonage was when a Japanese farmer, with a few acres of vegetable farm within hours away from Seattle, hired me. In most of my time as a stoop-laborer, I toiled from sunrise to sunset under all kinds of weather with my hands and mostly on my knees. Machine-based agriculture was still very much a dream in those days. But this farmer offered me more than just work. Outside the workplace, I was treated like a member of the family. We partook of the same meals, enjoyed the evenings like family, and exchanged views and ideas like equals. Unfortunately, agriculture was, and still is, a seasonal enterprise. The weather eventually turned, and the farm work had to hibernate for the winter.

Snow fell into mountains and many daring men were recruited to clear the way for the trains to continue their course. The railroad tracks—of which I labored previously to lay—were covered by snow and had to be cleared to guarantee safe transportation. For weeks, I shoveled and shoveled snow until I could no longer endure the freezing temperatures.

After the fish cannery season ended, most of us, especially those who ventured to acquire higher education, would converge in the Yakima Valley to lend a helping hand in the gathering of the hops, a necessary ingredient in the brewing of liquor. The short harvest season conveniently fit in between school terms and gave students an opportunity to earn supplemental funds. Those who were not students would tarry longer in Yakima to gather the famous Washington apples which were then ready for harvesting.

One year coming back from Alaska, I teamed up with a crew which was contracted to "top" sugar beets, a crop abundantly grown in Montana. That particular year, a unique one indeed, was exceptionally cold. Snow arrived early that season, although we still had several acres of sugar beets untopped. We had to fulfill our obligation as embodied in our signed agreement; otherwise, we had to forfeit our hard-earned wages. Knee deep in snow and sometimes under whipping wintery winds, we descended onto the fields to finish our commitment. There were mornings when we awoke to find the cold white stuff under our cot beds. Welcome relief came when we discovered that another labor crew in the neighborhood agreed to lend us a hand. We finally accomplished our commitment, to our great relief, then we scattered in all directions. I looked into the possibility of working in the mine fields of Butte, Montana, but the idea of working miles underground scared me no end. I chose to seek my fortune in! sunny California.

By 1929, the Great Depression forced me to abandon my earnest desire to acquire any higher education. Work of any kind was sparse and looking for a job was like looking for a needle in a haystack. California agricultural labor was the only available alternative. Filipino labor was also preferred by the farmers and growers.

As the sun spends the winter in southern California, so was farm labor trekking to that territory. For adventure and mostly to find available work, I teamed up with a few friends to seek the pot of gold in the Imperial Valley. Under pine trees, near canals flowing with Colorado River water, we camped. Kerosene lamps and flickering candles were our standard illumination, by which we augmented those offered by Mother Nature, the moon and the stars. Reeds and bushes were tied together to build enclosures for a little privacy, for nature's call or for baths. Makeshift rock stoves or small ditches in the ground were our cooking tools. Conditions were primitive indeed, yet we had to survive. Work included covering cantaloupe seedlings to safeguard them from freezing or picking peas. Later, lettuce and carrots were sown, grown, and then harvested.

As the Great Depression settled into the land, the carrot fields became overmanned. We had to struggle and fight for areas to work. There were quarrels and verbal confrontations; however, nothing of disastrous results happened. Those who, by choice or unforeseen circumstances, could stand the 100+ degree heat would remain in the Imperial Valley to pick and pack tomatoes or cantaloupes. Others would move on to other work.

Through these unforeseen and uncontrollable events, my crew was once placed in this predicament. After discussing our options, we bid *adieu* to our farmer employer, and with all our worldly belongings packed and loaded in our dilapidated automobiles, we pointed our compasses north to the Guadalupe-Santa Maria area to help harvest the carrots grown there. We filled our tanks (six cars) with fuel. But instead of heading directly to our intended destination, the lure of gambling rerouted us to the lure of gambling in the south of the border city, Mexicali. The get-rich quick syndrome robbed us of our better judgment. Synchronizing our watches, we all agreed to leave by 7 p.m., in order to make breakfast in Los Angeles. So south we went, hoping and praying to find a pot of gold at the end of the rainbow. However, the odds were stacked high against us, and consequently, we wound up totally embarrassed, humiliated, and without the shirts off our backs. We could not even muster among us the price of gas needed to reach our intended destination.

We had no alternative but to remain in the sultry Imperial Valley and seek summer employment. Slowly and hesitantly, we traced our route back to the ranch where we bid *adieu* just a few hours ago. We woke up the gentleman farmer and begged him to take us back as his ranch hands. Without hesitation, he accepted us; he knew us as trusted employees and he did not want to bother finding other hands.

We went to work harvesting his already ripe, succulent cantaloupes. That summer—every day of it—was boiling hot. You could fry an egg on the sidewalk. The sun was burning our skins; we shed gallons of sweat daily. The worst part of this experience, however, was the lack of ready cash to buy our daily sustenance. We, therefore, tightened our belts and, believe it or not, we were able to maintain our sanity while feasting on cantaloupe for breakfast, lunch, and dinner—for three days. At the end of the three days of this unusual diet, we were able to draw advanced pay. We then enjoyed a delicious meal of rice, meal, fish, and vegetables. With this very unusual and odd experiences, I vowed never to return to toil under these unsuitable living conditions of the Imperial Valley. When the season was over, we travelled to the agriculture-rich Santa Maria Valley, then to the grape ranches of Fresno. The cycle repeated itself year in and out—migratory farming to the core.

There were times when I would leave farm work and go to the cities to find work. Therefore, when I came to Salinas in 1935, many of the crew bosses and farm laborers did not believe that I could handle strenuous stoop labor. A cousin of mine, for whom I was able to finance his way to this country, was toiling in the Salinas Valley. He had hoped to be able to financially aid his sisters back home. At one time I joined him at his campsite. He also did not believe I could cope with the farm work, so I had to prove once again that I could keep up with the crew harvesting lettuce.

Then one day, we finished cutting lettuce before lunch time. The straw boss, then, announced that those who wanted to bunch carrots could be deployed in the carrot patches after lunch. Most of the men worked in pairs at this endeavor, one to clean the carrot tops of extra yellowed leaves, and the other to bunch them according to size and the required approximate weight. I asked my cousin if he would pair up with me, but he flatly. In fact, not one of the crew would consider me as an acceptable partner, a slight that kept me smiling on the inside, though quite hurt on the outside.

We went to bunch carrots that afternoon. Before the truck that brought us even stopped, most of the laborers were already staking territories for them to work. I was the last one off the truck, and the lesser, unclaimed territory became my charge. We bunched and bunched, crated our bundles as prescribed, and then at dusk, we were ready to go back to camp. As was the custom, you were paid by the amount of work you accomplished. There was a designated number of bunches per box and a price for a box, so for accounting purposes, it was appropriately advisable lo just record the number of boxes.

On the way home inside the truck, within hearing distance to every member of the crew, the straw boss was tallying the sum of our work. He went through his roster and by design perhaps, or by other consideration, he placed me last. When he came to me, he whispered, "Ading, how many boxes have you filled today?" I knew what the others had made; I knew the capabilities of all of them. Then to his surprise and to the amazement of the entire crew, I stated loudly my accomplishment. I did more than most of those working in teams and outbunched their acclaimed champion by four boxes. To disprove their doubts, I suggested that we go back and fully account my claim. They didn't know that I had been bunching carrots in Santa Maria, Guadalupe, and Lompoc, places where you could meet some of the champion carrot bunchers in all of California. I gained their respect then. And they also learned, including my blood cousin, not to judge a book by its cover.

In the mid-1930s, I again came to Salinas to find work, but winter and the rains kept the fields untilled and Filipinos in the labor camps idle. These labor camp operators had one commendable contribution to their men. They had established credit accounts with food marts, so to keep their men, they also gave food credits to be paid when work was available. Their main and foremost fear was that some of their men might jump camp, thus leaving him with uncollectible accounts. But life is a gamble, and this was the stake they had lo bet on.

With competition with several agents and business standing still, I was urged by a newly acquired friend to go live with him at a labor camp within walking distance from town. I traded my position as a made-to-measure suit connector for farm work. During that period of time, Filipino men splurged on fancy made-to-measure suits; ready-made ones were out of vogue, likewise, jackets and sweaters. A Filipino going to town, wearing anything but a made-to-measure suit would be the object of continued ridicule by his peers. The gospel truth—which was even acknowledged by the local press—was that if you wanted to see the latest men's fashion attire, go see the Filipinos.

I went to join the gang at the labor camp, welcomed heartily by the men, but the labor boss had reservations. He made it very plain that I and another companion were not programmed for farm work; that we were just seasoned *bolacbols*.[44] His feelings were open and he, at times, was at odds with my friend, Bob, who brought us to camp. We endured the insinuations and never even discussed it with the gang. Life went on without diffusing the allegations. We suffered a couple of months of wet weather—meaning no work and an accumulated food account—the rains and inclement weather gave way to the sun, and farm activities began again to spring to life.

The thinning of lettuce was the order of the day. Bob and I shyly approached the boss to please bear with us and instruct us on the technique of using the short hoe. We wanted to impress him that we were ready and willing to learn. The first day, he told us to watch studiously how his seasoned workers performed. Later, he assigned us our own rows to thin, him with eagle eyes, instructing us, helping us keep abreast with the others. We watched him with interest, asking questions and appearing eager to learn the mysteries of the task. We surely made him earn his keep that morning.

Farm work was a back-breaking activity. To relieve the worker from stress and stamina, it was an accepted practice to give the workers a ten- to fifteen-minute break in the middle of the morning and afternoon. During our break time, Bob and I amusingly agreed to inform the boss to free us from his watchful eyes and just us do our assigned chores at our leisure. Not only that, but we issued a challenge to all his seasoned helpers to race us with no strings attached. The boss and the other crew members were stunned by our challenging proclamation. It was then that we demonstrated our previously acquired skills in the thinning of the green gold. It came to pass that nobody, even the straw boss, could keep up with us in speed, neatness, and accuracy. During the lunch hour in front of the entire crew, the boss publicly apologized to us for all the things he said against us, admitting that it was not fair to judge someone by looks only. Performance is the true measure of one's ability.

What these men didn't know was that Bob and I had extensive experience thinning lettuce in the Imperial Valley and Arizona, and that we were often contracted and paid by the acre. To make money by the acre meant that you had beat hourly wages. Simply put, you had to "work like hell."

However, there was one problem that arose relative to our thinning position. While we were thinning around the rest of the crew, we would occasionally lie down to rest, sometimes on the end of the field opposite the end where the rest were grouped. The owner of the farm noticed the situation, perhaps by binoculars, and complained to our straw boss about the two "lazy bums" leisurely goofing off during work. The straw boss explained the situation, but the owner entertained some doubts. But he was eventually satisfied after he actually spied on us through his binoculars.

A good comradeship and brotherly understanding grew and developed amongst most camp personnel. Benny, the one who brought me to this particular labor camp, and I became very good pals. We loved each other's company. We went places together. We even bought a car together. It was at this place that I launched my plan to organize the farm workers, in an effort to improve living conditions. Benny was with me altogether through thick or thin. The 1936 Labor Strike found me part and parcel of this work crew.

Not many moons passed following the War in Salinas[45] when some folks in camp decided to pool together our meager cash assets with the straw boss to invest their capital and organize the Philippine Trading Company, a merchandising concern dealing with the needs of the working men. We opened shop in the heart of Chinatown in Salinas. The building we leased had a frontage store with rooms at the back to house every member of the crew. However, the services of each business partner were not essential in the store operation, so most of us continued to work for the farmers, who needed experienced workers.

The greatest miracle happened to Benny and me during our friendship. One lonely night in 1937, while we wasted precious time patronizing the pool halls and the Chinese gambling dens, we heard missionaries preaching their dogmas from a street comer. What they were expounding did not in the least attract us, for we did not believe what they were heartily impressing upon unbelieving crowd. But what caught our attention was the youthfulness and features of these missionaries—all three of them. We learned later that they were sisters, all in their early twenties. Believe it or not, we followed them to their revival meetings with the expectancy of getting to know them more personally, nay, intimately, if possible.

That meeting marked the omega of all my lost weekends and the alpha of becoming a born-again Christian. We attended many of their revival meetings. We socialized and participated in church activities. I got better acquainted with these charming missionaries and as the days passed, I began to review my past. As I looked back, I commenced to realize the fruitlessness of my life. I felt ashamed of myself. A complicated hostility prevailed within me. What had I done to my life? What does the future hold in store for me? Is it advantageous to turn a new leaf, start a new life? In the privacy of my room, I found myself reprimanding my super ego, accounting my weaknesses, my spineless behaviors, my undue submission to the destructive influences abundantly manifested around me.

I regretted those lost years of my life, the years spent

foolishly and unfruitfully, the spineless years of my gambling, drinking, and succumbing to a great many sinful ways.[46] And I had completely cut off my connections to my family in the homeland. I was aware they wanted to know if I was still alive, what I had been doing, and why all communication had been cut off. I learned of these concerns from townmates who received inquiring communications, the same kind of communications I also had the honor of receiving. But what my relatives in the homeland didn't know was that there was a silent and solemn understanding amongst us in the states that "he who is without sin cast the first stone."

Eventually, I swallowed my pride and again renewed communications with my family. But when my family opened their hearts to accept me back, without any grueling third degrees, it was one of the happiest moments of my life. It shocked them though, to learn that I was I alive, for they had already written me off as dead. They had even sanctioned the nine-day Novena in my memory, a prevalent ritual that Filipino Catholics practiced and solemnized. So I had sort of risen from the dead.

I came to understand that, when I was a "living dead," I was so ashamed that I had failed them, that I preferred for them to believe I was dead than have them know that I was what I was. My life was worse than a Filipino movie without a plot.

But starting a new lease on my life was a tortuous route to follow. Pressures from my peers, temptations thrown in my face, lures and traps designed lo trip me, offers of the easy life around me, were all factors I had to conquer. But I surmounted all these hurdles. After all, I had publicly confessed before many people and before my God that I had sinned, sinned, and sinned, and that I also publicly proclaimed that I was a new man—born-again into a life, adversely and contrary to my life in sin. I had to stand strictly and positively to my vow. And to that end, I rededicated my life.

Oddly, I lost my dignity and self-respect in the Chinatowns of California, but I regained them back living at the center of Chinatown, in Salinas.

The Good Book admonishes us: “If they throw you stones, throw them bread. If they slap you on one cheek, turn also the other cheek.”

5. THE FILIPINO COMMUNITY CONNECTION

For as long as I can remember, my dad was involved in many different civic organizations and worked tirelessly in volunteer government service. As a child, I remember many evenings when he would cook us dinner, then announce that he had a meeting to go to. (Of course, as my mom worked swing shift at the hospital, this allowed us to watch TV during school nights!) I think it was because he had a conviction, deeply marbled in his flesh, that one must stand up for justice and equality and righteousness. I firmly believe that the most productive period of his life, and also the most rewarding, was after he retired. Because he could fully devote himself to the service of others, which he loved to do.

I left the Philippines by choice, but nobody has been able to take the Philippines away from me, or out of me. I may have been naturalized an American citizen, yet the color of my skin remains brown. I still think, talk, and act as a Filipino.

Not long after the surrender of the Japanese at the end of World War II, I decided to get out of the US Armed Forces Military Intelligence Division, which was attached to the Air Force.[47] We Filipino soldiers fought for the freedom which society denied us, fought for the liberty that excluded us, and for the democracy that always evaded us. Now, I came back to Salinas hoping to pick up the life I had left behind. But the world had become quite different than the life I had left.

Friends I knew traveled to other regions, perhaps to greener pastures; others opted to become professional soldiers, seeing the world and ready to fight other wars. Even our business venture had suffered due to the shortage of merchandise, and with the opening of a new shopping center in downtown Salinas. Even my own wardrobe of clothing, which I had entrusted to my pals when I was called to serve, were no longer waiting for me. So I could not discard my army outfit, for there were no clothes available in the stores immediately after the war. Several months elapsed before I could buy myself civilian clothing, so my army uniform had to be dyed into other colors to separate myself from the Armed Forces.

Beyond my attempts to resuscitate our business, I accepted the task of organizing a new American Legion post in our area: Fil-Am Post 652.[48] After the war, many Filipino veterans joined the American Legion, and I was also invited to join one of the local posts. But I hesitated to join, because I found out that the Filipinos were not integrally accepted during meetings. They segregated themselves and were not participating in any of the Post's activities. I was aware of the existence of Filipino-American Legion Posts like the Manila Post in Los Angeles and the Leyte Post in San Diego. So I requested and was granted permission to form Fil-Am Post 652 in Salinas. I reasoned that becoming a separate Post enabled Filipinos to more comprehensively act for ourselves and to fully participate in the affairs and programs of the American Legion.[49] Thankfully, the 13th District Officers were helpful to guide me and get organized.

As I was actively coping with these tasks, I was jolted by a proposition presented to me by several of my former ideological enemies. The then incumbent president, his co-officers and other leaders of the Filipino Community of Salinas Valley approached me, offering me the top leadership of the organization. This was surprising to me because this group and I didn't see eye-to-eye on many important issues of the period—including farm workers unionization and the American citizenship of Filipinos. Regarding the latter, I was a dedicated member of the Committee for the Protection of the Foreign Born, and I had campaigned for the inclusion of Filipinos as a group eligible for American citizenship. They opposed this position based on their belief that only "traitors" would change citizenship.[50] In addition, I was well known for leading the Salinas strike of 1936, so I was not accepted by this community, who fought for the preservation of labor bosses.

All these people were now coming to me, urging me to take over the leadership of the FCSV, despite them campaigning hard to defeat me when I offered my services before World War II. So, there was a compelling reason for me to not readily accept their proposition. The increasing pressures upon me, both personal and business-wise, as well as the organization of a local Filipino Post of the American Legion were all strong reasons for my hesitation. On the other hand, my vision for assisting my people was a persistent and undeniable influence. Finally, I succumbed to their continual insistence and acceded to their clamor.

Within two short months after becoming a civilian, at a meeting of the FCSV, I was installed as president of the association. No elaborate ceremony, no fanfare. Serving with me as vice-president was Benny Espejo,[51] who operated a restaurant located at the heart of Chinatown. The treasurer owned and operated a grocery store at the edge of Chinatown. My secretary was a student at Hartnell College, and a sister-in-law of the treasurer.

The Chinatown[52] *pinoys*, all residents of the "Boulevard of broken dreams," had now taken over management of the FCSV.

◆ ◆ ◆

The most obvious misstep of the previous administration —and a great shock to us—was the total lack of past records. There were no Constitution and By-Laws, no financial accounts, no papers, no pencils, not a single penny—nothing whatsoever to relate to previous activities. They simply passed down to us the title, "Filipino Community of Salinas Valley."

As business people, we proved ourselves up to the task. Our first step was to call for a membership meeting. Meetings were then held at the Filipino Presbyterian Church in Salinas. At this meeting, we presented these problems to the membership. But to solve these problems, we needed financial backing to operate the association. To show that we meant business, all the new officers generously fed the kitty, and along with other donations, the result was favorably outstanding. Then we appointed committees from volunteers. The most important committees appointed were a committee to draft our Constitution and By-Laws and a financial committee to raise additional funds. These two committees vowed to be ready to submit reports within two weeks. Enthusiasm was high amongst these volunteers. By the early part of 1946, our Constitution and By-Laws was ready for adoption and the membership overwhelmingly accepted it with very few modifications. The financial committee was also able to raise sufficient funds to keep the FCSV in operation.

There were traditions and commitments of the FCSV that needed perpetuations. An annual Queen Contest, a good money-raising activity, had to be continued, so a committee was named to manage it. The contest usually was held in June to coincide with the California Rodeo. At the contest, the Queen and her Princesses were publicly crowned, and they adorned our lighted float during the annual parade at the annual California Rodeo held in Salinas.

The year 1946 proved to be a monumental year for Filipinos everywhere. On July 4 of that year, the stars and stripes were forever lowered on Philippine soil, and in its place, the Philippine flag was raised.[53] Those of us who were then American citizens were doubly elated and very happy for our double status during that special day. As American citizens, we were granting independence to our homeland, and as Filipinos, we were being elevated as an independent nation.

We in Salinas, particularly the members of the FCSV, decided to make that day a very memorable day, and we made elaborate preparations for that event. In fact, our celebration lasted two days. The first day was devoted to honoring our Filipino Community Queen and her Royal Court. The Salinas Armory, the best and largest available building in the Salinas Valley, was the scene of the royal ceremonies. The following day, we had our flag raising activities, an all-day free steak and chicken barbecue picnic, and softball and volleyball tournaments, all held at the Sherwood Picnic Grounds in Salinas.

We were grateful to the City of Salinas for preparing for us an elevated platform for our program and for erecting two poles to hoist both the American and Filipino flags. Fresh from the wars, members of the American Legion Fil-Am Post, in which I presided as Commander,[54] did the honor of raising the flags with honor and dignity. The athletic contests attracted teams from the Santa Maria, San Luis Obispo, and Stockton areas. Prizes were awarded to all athletic teams that honored us with their participation. Our finance committee did a commendable job of raising funds to meet all the necessary expenses. To our knowledge, no other Filipino Community in the whole continental United States did top, nay, equal, our celebration.

◆ ◆ ◆

After the cessation of hostilities in the Pacific, many of the "little brown soldiers"[55] were coming "home" to re-enter civilian life. The FCSV, realizing their exclusion from the welcome mat which honored others belonging to other races, conceived a plan to welcome these ex-GIs home. We decided that a ball and banquet at the Salinas Armory, free to the soldiers and open to all the civilian population, was an appropriate celebration.

The City of Salinas watched with favor this planned welcome party. A local community leader, Judge Brasil, who served as District Attorney in Monterey County and later served as Superior Court Judge—and who never accepted any of the many invitations by the FCSV—surprised us by attending this welcome shindig. In fact, he went so far as to welcome each and every soldier by helping us award certificates of appreciation to some four hundred ex-GIs. That occasion was his only appearance in Filipino community activities. Our Filipino Community once again scored a success. And there were many more to come.

◆ ◆ ◆

Over time, I began to realize that, prior to our group taking the reins, the FCSV was a stagnant and inert organization. It had been sick to the core, lying, not moving in bed, with no signs of an iota of energy. No wonder those who manned it were eager and determined to pass the helm to some unsuspecting, untried leaders. Thankfully, we were able to inject a healthy new adrenalin into the association with the result being a rejuvenated community.

When you dream, dream big. When I first accepted the office as president, one of the propositions I openly suggested —and one which was readily and unanimously accepted by my colleagues—was the audacious goal of erecting a building for the exclusive use of the Filipino community.

Thus, it was mutually agreed that some part of all the finances raised for the FCSV be set aside for this goal. This project became a sort of a dream for me, inspired by my meetings with Filipinos in other parts of the country during my tour of duty as an American soldier. In Chicago, Detroit, New York, Brooklyn, Philadelphia, Washington DC, and other cities, I had attended various Filipino functions at impressive meeting halls. But in Salinas, it was a constant problem to find a place to celebrate our programs and hold dances. Though there were several venues available to rent, it was always a problem to get the proper date or the right time. So, the dream for a Filipino community building was set in motion. Three years after the plan was launched, the FCSV purchased its first lot. In seven years, we were able to acquire three adjoining lots, enough space to build our dream building.

Building designs, plans, and blueprints were prepared, licenses to build were acquired, and an eager contractor was hired. But our treasury had only a few hundred dollars to offer. We sought the help of local banks and lending institutions, but with the FCSV having no regular, steady income and unable to offer any concrete collateral, our efforts to produce financial assistance came up empty.

The incumbent President Benny Espejo and his co-officers never admitted defeat. Many alternatives to raise funds were discussed, but it would take years to earn and save the necessary monies. All but a few of our members wanted action—now or never. Out of the blue sky, an out-of-the-ordinary business idea was suggested. What if the home equities of several of the FCSV members was put up for collateral so that a bank loan would be granted? A strange, novel idea, indeed!

At that time, it was hardly possible for Filipinos to acquire real property. Restrictions, conditions, and many considerations prevented Filipinos from buying property. However, there were areas where these restrictions didn't affect Filipinos. One was for those few families who had children born in the US. They families were able to buy property under the names of their children, who were American citizens by birth. It took great and elaborate persuasions, compromises, and dedications, but in the end, a handful of families agreed to put up their homes as collateral for a bank loan. It was a victory of the FCSV, and we were grateful for the sacrifices and dedication of these very, very trusting families, who mortgaged their private homes for the sake of the FCSV and for the Filipino cause.

The building became a joyful reality, a real symbol of pride and unity of the Filipino people in the Salinas Valley.[56] The edifice on Lake Street in Salinas, having been completed and furnished mostly by donations from those who cared, became the very center of all Filipino activities. Weddings, parties, programs, dinners, benefit dances, and fund-raising activities were common events at the facility. The Filipino Community, however, took priority for their activities. The Legionarios Del Trabajo with its seven lodges, the Tarlakenians, the Narvakenians, the Pangasinans, The First and Second Filipino Regiments Association, Fil-Am Post 652, and other Filipino groups or individuals all made the building their home.

It became very important and necessary that the FCSV

schedule the orderly use of the building in advance. So at the beginning of each new year, a meeting of all the leaders of every Filipino organization was convened to agree on scheduling dates for their yearly activities. This system, still strictly followed even now, eliminated conflicts, and encouraged a sense of unbiased cooperation among the many organizations in the Valley.

I had previously mentioned the California Rodeo.[57] Held in Salinas, the rodeo was a part of Salinas Big Week, which had been an annual local affair for many generations. It is a week of pleasure and fun not only for the town folk, but for thousands of visitors as well. Aside from the actual rodeo which attracts the best riders and cowboys from all over the country. Main Street in Salinas used to be a beehive of activities. It became a street of commodity booths, stalls displaying arts and crafts, and food concessions. The FCSV and Fil-Am Post 652 joined many local service associations in the display of products and foods to the pleasure and fun-loving citizens.

Saturday night of Big Week was the big magnet that attracted significant out-of-town participation. It was the night of the lighted parade. Beautiful floats, marching bands, drill teams, and other attractions marched through the streets of Salinas to the delight and joy of thousands of people. This night-lighted parade was acknowledged as the biggest night parade in the country.

Filipinos in the Salinas Valley had been part and parcel of the parade for many years, and the FCSV always entered a decorated float in the Saturday night extravaganza. Some of our floats earned commendations and trophies. There were years when the Filipinos were represented not only by the FCSV, but by the Caballeros de Dimasalang, who also entered their own float followed by their own sponsored drum and bugle corps composed of young Filipino children. The Filipino-American Citizens League of Monterey County, organized in 1946, also participated in the parade occasionally.

Unfortunately, the cost of participation and the weeks of preparation were reasons that these organizations curtailed further participation. The last time the FCSV put up a float, our young people volunteered to design, construct and run it. It was a beautiful creation, but it heavily taxed their imagination. I was the President when the FCSV last joined the parade in 1971. Succeeding executives of the FCSV were unable to continue the tradition. In addition, excessive drinking and fighting, which began to occur during the traditional all-night dancing on Main Street, were also contributing factors for the stoppage.

During Big Week, all citizens were expected to dress the part, either wearing a cowboy outfit or any part thereof. Failure to comply and venture into downtown areas, and you may be caught and imprisoned in the "hoosegow," a makeshift jail set up on Main Street. Pay a "fine" and you were set free. I ventured one day onto Main Street and was unwittingly nabbed for not being clad in cowboy garb. I was locked in the hoosegow for a few minutes but was freed without the usual fine. My plea was "I wasn't aware of the tradition."

It hurts to admit that although comradeship prevailed among the majority of Filipinos, there also existed antagonism among us as well. Strong loyalties were practiced among the tribes (Tagalog, Visaya, Ilocano, etc.), or in smaller groups based on city of origin (Morongs, Tanays, Vigan, Candon, or others). Each group tended to believe that when one was involved, the rest of the group was also hurt. For example, if a Morong was slightly antagonized by a Candon; not only was the individual Morong involved, but the entire Morong clan felt it as well. And rivalry between and among clans was rampant in those decades.

Another trait of the Filipino was their general lack of interest in problems or issues that affected them as a race or group. This may explain the lack of interest in joining clubs or associations, or the lack of interest and concern in the solution of national or racial problems. This kind of thinking prevails even at the present time. During the early years, when we called for a meeting of the FCSV, the vice-president and I would request —and even demand—that the gambling establishments close their doors for at least a few hours during that assemblage day. We succeeded in our threats at times but not always. "I have no time" or "I have no ride" were very common excuses, and yet, organize a cock-fight party or a gambling trip to Reno, and they would drop everything so they could participate.

In 1971, the Salinas Community Arts Council staged their annual International Culture Day. The FCSV received an invitation to participate, and being President at that time, we acknowledged with pride the invitation. The Filipino Community at that time was devoid of a cultural program. We simply had no active or organized cultural activities. There were in existence, however, trained Filipino children under the sponsorship of other Filipino clubs and associations.

The Laoaguenians[58] in Salinas, which I organized and served as President, had children trained in Philippine folk dancing. A cultural committee was hastily appointed, and these children were recruited to represent the FCSV.[59] During that Cultural Fair held at Hartnell College, different ethnic groups and races were assigned booths to display arts, artifacts, and products from their own homelands. Volunteers manned our booth, and artifacts which were borrowed from many households and from the Philippine stores were artfully displayed. Philippine native attire representing different periods and ages, the modern *Barong Tagalog*[60] and *Terno*[61] surprisingly took the spotlight. The Filipinos and Filipinas attending wore Philippine attire as well. The Filipino folk dances—including the *Tinikling* and *Pandango Sa Haw*—received the enthusiastic accolade of the audience. For songs, we were fortunate at that period to have in

Salinas a former radio and stage singing star from the homeland to render those ear-pleasing *kundimans*[62] from the *Pearl of the Orient Seas.*

From the success of that cultural experience, the FCSV campaigned for the inclusion of a cultural program in the many facets of our activities, aims and objectives. Filipino children were introduced to some aspect of their culture and heritage. They danced and sang in many cultural fairs. There were times when our group visited old people's homes and convalescent hospitals primarily to entertain with dance and song.

One rare recognition of the FCSV took place during one of my terms as chief executive officer of the FCSV. It has never been duplicated; it has not touched other racial or ethnic groups. When the State of California dedicated the grand opening of the Division of Motor Vehicles office building in Salinas, the FCSV was greatly honored when it was invited to present their ruling Miss Philippines to be their guest of honor. She, in her glowing Filipina dress, performed the ribbon-cutting ceremonies. It was a great honor for her and a public recognition of the FCSV.

Fort Ord, the Army installation in Monterey County, sponsored their annual Heritage Week. Fortunately, our county is blessed with the preponderance of many cultures. All ethnic groups were invited and urged to participate. Now, at the time, there were some thirty Filipino organizations, clubs, and associations in Monterey County, including four community clubs. The Filipino Community of Salinas, though not the closest to Fort Ord, represented Monterey County. The food booth was a feature of our participation, in addition to the folk dancing and singing programs. Since that time, *lumpia*[63] and *pansit,*[64] favorite foods of the Filipino people at home and abroad, have now become synonymous to the Filipino, just as chop suey is to the Chinese, sushi to the Japanese, or the taco and burrito to the Mexican people.

The Filipino Cultural Program of the FCSV has now grown and developed to the point that their services are not only limited to our area but have started to influence other regions. The growth of this program and its enlightened impact to the community has also entitled them to receive grants from philanthropic establishments.

There was a time during one of my incumbency periods when we encountered a financial shortfall at FCSV. It was not that we could not meet our financial obligations. Far from that status, the problem was that we failed to raise sufficient funds to repaint the inside of the building. This unfortunate situation became the issue which I, as President, and a prominent Filipino doctor had a heated misunderstanding. This doctor—who cherished exploding into criticisms, but never, never voluntarily offered a penny—offered to entertain his social-service colleagues at the Filipino Community Hall. But he knew first-hand the current condition of the structure. After his party, he lambasted me for the "unpresentative" condition of the hall. He deliberately exhibited to his friends the dirty linens of the community to downgrade his own people perhaps, but I believe he succeeded in embarrassing and humiliating himself.

After that incident, I begged for help from the members of the corporation. But that was the busy work-season of our *paisanos*. So, my family—my wife and my four preteen sons and I —took reign of the occasion. I purchased the necessary tools and appropriate paints and the Luz clan, sleeves rolled, went to work. The family, not being professional painters, did their darnest best to make the building look more presentable.[65] Some criticized us for doing the laborious task; others even laughed at us, but the work was done at no expense to the FCSV.

Another happening—not an act of man, but a disaster uncontrollable by humans—occurred during the presidency of Jose Mendoza. It was a disastrous surprise. One day, the building custodian opened the front door and found himself stepping into a sunken floor. The foyer and front side of the floor just caved in. Luckily, it did not happen when people were around. The actual explanation of the destruction by the crew that made the repairs was that the original contractor failed to solidify the base prior to laying the floor. It must be recalled that Lake Street (now Calle Cebu) was at one time an actual watery lake. There was no ready cash to make immediate repairs, so we had to resort to the only alternative, borrowing the necessary amount from the bank. We had an A-1 rating then, and the loan was paid in due time. The repairs were done satisfactorily; it is until now in good, proper solid condition.

◆ ◆ ◆

The FCSV enjoyed some of its most prosperous years during my last terms as Chief Executive in 1981-1984. In those years, the FCSV was at the height of a financial upheaval. Its annual budget topped $90,000. The economic picture was rosy and bright. We had donated and shared our financial largesse to the tune of many thousands of dollars to several public service organizations. To name a few: the American Red Cross, the Community Chest, Salinas Valley Memorial Hospital,[66] local churches, and earthquake or flood victims in this nation and in the Philippines and Mexico. In addition, we established separate solvent funds for: the General Fund; Building and Grounds Fund; Death Benefit Fund;[67] Scholarship Fund;[68] an interest-free Student Loan Fund; a Cultural Fund; and a Senior Citizens Fund.

A senior citizen's luncheon program continued to be an on-going activity of the FCSV. At these luncheons—twice monthly on the first Wednesday of the month—participants paid a minimal fee of 50 cents (the third Wednesday of the month was completely free to all who attended). During these senior luncheon days, aside from the games played and the dances enjoyed, volunteer Filipino nurses offered free blood pressure checks to all. The Monterey County Health Department sent a crew of four or five health care professionals (SCAN) to render free service to the seniors. And the Monterey Alliance of Aging also sent a representative to advise and inform the seniors of problems and benefits affecting them.

One other feature of special mention was the recognition of the FCSV for the value of time of service rendered by the Executive Board. Every member of the Board was assigned a committee to chair, and he/she became fully responsible to fulfill faithfully and diligently the demands of the assignment. Each committee had budgeted accounts to run its program. Since the FCSV was, so to speak, flowing in honey, all Board members received an additional per diem of $30.00 for every meeting attended.

Since we organized the FCSV in late 1936, I have never decreased my interest and dedication to this association. I have served in many capacities, having been its president for many terms, in aggregate over ten years. I freely gave my time as a paralegal member, having written all the contracts and legal papers required in connection with the programs of the FCSV. This included lease/rent contracts, contest contracts, and loans and other banking contracts. I also personally tackled the task of incorporating FCSV with the State of California in 1954 to gain non-profit status. I have served the FCSV in many capacities since its organization in 1936—from president to legal representative to painter and renovator. I do believe I am the only one who can claim that distinction.

One of the greatest contributions I rendered to the organization was the addition to the old building. Although plans for such an addition was conceived by my predecessor, the whole plan was completed during my last years as president. We, nevertheless, encountered several roadblocks by city regulations and restrictions. Such requirements had to be hurdled before building permits were issued. Necessary changes were made to the building blueprints, since parts of the old structure had to be updated to conform to city construction codes, and parking spaces had to be provided to fulfill city requirements.

Working together with the city people, we finally arrived at an agreement which complied with all building codes and requirements. We hired a licensed Filipino building contractor (we had to patronize our own) and soon, work was initiated. In the middle of the construction, for reasons beyond our control and not fully within community comprehension, the contractor vanished, never to re-appear again. Luckily, the contract we signed protected the FCSV's interests, and no loss other than time was incurred. Another contractor was approached, and he consented to finish the job to the full satisfaction of the FCSV and the city inspectors.

The Community Hall had been the target of vandalism for many years. Windows were frequently broken, doors were smashed, and the building was frequently looted. Many nights, mostly at dawn, I would be called by the local police to meet them at the hall to evaluate and account for all the losses. Televisions, fruits, candies, cigarettes, and food were the most notable losses. Office files were in disarray, probably in search of cash. This was an on-going problem, not only because of constant repairs, but because our overall building insurance rose to prohibitive amounts. To minimize this kind of problem, we installed iron bars on the windows, double locks on the doors, and limited the number of key holders to the doors of the building. Tables and chairs were properly imprinted with the name of the FCSV for security and identification. Finally, before I left office, I made certain that the ladies comfort room was doubled in size, and that the parking lot was repaved.

During the passing of the gavel ceremonies, my administration was proud to leave the office in a good financial position even as we, at that night, doled out thousands of dollars to charity. The different funds were securely intact; authentic records were clear and positively accurate and were handed down to my successor. My memento for my services was a travelling bag, a send-away. Can you imagine that?

The succeeding administrations took different routes from mine. Their programs and methods of operation demonstratively were adverse from their predecessors. Soon, the FCSV was running on deficits and within four years, the corporation was financially in the scarlet red.

The most dramatic development, to my own observation and knowledge, was the differences between the type of people responsible to administrate the affairs of the FCSV. Starting from my last stint as FCSV President all the way back to the beginning, most all of the elected officers, including the members of the Board of Directors, were agricultural workers, most of them with lowly elementary education. They knew from personal experience the many adversities that set upon us, and they knew the real importance of oneness. They were products of the school of hard knocks. These non-professionals were cautious conservatives who were, however, ready, willing, and able to make sacrifices. Those who succeeded me—those who took over the reins of the FCSV—were mostly college-educated professionals like lawyers, medical doctors, engineers, and teachers. These professionals were liberals who, in my opinion, cared more for their professions than for the good of the FCSV.

◆ ◆ ◆

Presently, in 1995, the FCSV is in a grave financial shortfall. Not only is it financially broke, the FCSV has also lost its tax-exempt status. Existing rules and regulations were completely ignored, city ordinances were not complied with, California Franchise Tax laws were totally shelved, records of the association became personal property of the responsible officers, and financial accounts were intermingled. The unfortunate truth is that the FCSV is in debt to the estimated tune of about $50,000. That is the mystic gospel truth—a very grave problem in every sense.

The FCSV is presently unstable and far from being free from seeming bankruptcy. The incumbent president, Art Sabiniano, acquired a huge headache but he is giving it his best shot. He started to straighten out some problems—unpaid insurance and existing bank loans were paid off, and necessary repairs on the building were made. But the problems linger. I have complete confidence that the FCSV will thrive and rise again. There is no doubt that the elected officials and members, working together, will withstand any catastrophe that may appear.

6. POLITICAL CONNECTIONS

I remember running for student body president in the sixth grade. Of course, I was not running because of any need to be in charge or make a difference. In my own way, I was just trying to be like my dad. Unfortunately, running against me was Billy Dobbs, the very popular, blue-eyed, blonde-haired Little League jock. I didn't stand a chance. I remember being more than disappointed. I felt the weight of unfairness that eventually comes to us all when reality hits you in the face. Life is hard. And so is politics.

My dad knew this. But he also knew that politics was one of the primary ways that social change could be instigated and instituted. So he spent much of his life involved in local politics—dozens and dozens of commissions, committees, boards, and organizations, as well as personally with many influential politicos and politicians. And at the end of his life, I think he believed that he had made a difference in the world. I believe he did as well.

On rare occasions, Filipino events required a larger hall than the FCSV could offer. Such an event, which attracted the Filipino elites and assorted social cream aspirants in Salinas and Monterey areas, sprung up in 1957. This dinner/dance, presented at the Salinas Armory, was a swanky affair. Bejeweled ladies proudly displayed their best evening attire—the butterfly-sleeved Filipina dresses and the latest modern styles, and men attired in lacy embroidered barongs or in rented tuxedos. It was an affair that filled the Armory Hall wall-to-wall with competing proud Filipino citizenry.

The most notable and distinguished guest of the evening was the Honorable Fred Farr, the incumbent state senator from Monterey County. His arrival at the Armory was eagerly anticipated as it seemed that all the so-called leaders, gentlemen and ladies alike, were constantly watching the front entrance for his appearance. When he finally showed up at the door, he was literally mobbed. Ladies and gentlemen rushed to greet him, hoping to shake his political hands. My future wife, Cresencia, then a new addition to our society, amusingly watched the circus-like activity. She looked at me, wondering why I did not make any effort to meet our distinguished guest. In obvious thought, she finally burst out, "Why are you not with the mob to greet the Senator?"

I kind of expected her puzzled position; she may had anticipated her beau to be an eager part and parcel of the obviously eager crowd meeting the distinguished visitor, our honored guest. In reply to her question, I just jokingly replied, "If Mohammed cannot go to the mountain, let the mountain go to Mohammed."

Surely without doubt, she was taken aback by my impudent answer. But what came next was more shocking.

The Senator was led into the hall to the side opposite where Cres and I were seated. When he noticed me, he gracefully crossed the hall, the crowd watching his every movement, and came up to me and greeted me like an equal—like a lost brother, a friend, a confidant. The face of Cres suddenly showed great amazement. Those nearby who witnessed the drama were equally surprised as to why a senator would excuse himself from many admirers and cross an empty floor to meet a man seemingly waiting for a pleasant time of friendly tete-a-tete with him.

Naturally for my dear wife, her amazement meeting the distinguished senator deserved background explanation. Only a few people knew that our relationship—Fred and I—dated back to the days when he was a struggling young lawyer in the Monterey Peninsula. In 1947, he was appointed by the court to defend a Filipino accused of shooting and murdering in cold blood five of his Filipino co-workers during an unexpected altercation arising from a "friendly" card game. Their residence, furnished by their employer, was the bottom floor of a Class-A restaurant located on Highway 1, south of Carmel By-The-Sea. Playing cards was a kind of recreation culinary workers enjoyed after a hectic day in the pits. Filipino kitchen workers were abundantly employed by restaurants, cafes, and clubs in the Monterey Bay area.

After Fred Farr, the then lawyer, accepted the difficult and laborious task of defending the accused murderer (who obviously could not afford a lawyer himself), he sought the advice of anyone who knowledgeably understood the traits, lives, and preferences of the Filipino. His search led to my door, and a new partnership—and friendship—was then born. My responsibilities included helping him understand the Filipino, from their inside and outside feelings, to their ethnic characteristics. In short, he wanted to know intimately the Filipino. Another part of my responsibility was to evaluate the panel of jurors, who would sit in judgment of the alleged murderer. The case finally went to trial, jury empaneled, and Fred Farr made an strong defense, which ended in a life sentence with the possibility of parole. This was despite the prosecutors strongly demanding the death penalty, considering the severity of the crime—after all, five people died with the gun wielded by the defendant. It was a tremendous triumph for the defense, indeed!

So, while our mutual greeting surprised and amazed all who witnessed the scene, it was no surprise to me. And to Cres, she surely was very proud of her unassuming husband.

◆ ◆ ◆

The friendly and amicable relationship between Fred and I continued to the days of our retirements, when he decided, under the pressure and urging of his friends, to enter the political arena. He never failed to include me in his catalog of supporters. He would attend regular meetings of the Filipino American Citizens League,[69] a group designed to more or less inform, direct, and translate to the new citizens their new-found duties and responsibilities. Issues of the day were minutely studied and extensively discussed during these meetings. Farr not only elucidated the issues, but also revealed to us the legal implications of current issues. He also personally made himself available to many Filipino community functions. He became not only my friend, he became a friend of the Filipinos.

Also joining Farr was another local politician, a local rancher who later became a California state assemblyman, Alan Pattee. He also became a close friend of the Filipinos, simulating the movements of Fred Farr—attending Filipino functions and events, giving us political guidance, and making us aware of the ramifications of the issues of the times. The two became friendly antagonists in the political arena, both ardently vying for the support of the Filipino block. Both were endorsed by the valley Pinoys—Alan Pattee became a state assemblyman and Fred Farr served as state senator. While both were in Sacramento representing their constituents and districts, communications between me and them were frequent. When they came to our area during and between sessions, or when they needed to report to their constituents, I was never excluded from their invitations. To me, the present politicians in our own district could never match the concern and friendship to Filipinos of Fred Farr and the late Alan Pattee, who succumbed prematurely in a car accident on his way to report to us, his constituents.

There were other politicians in our district, nay, even elsewhere in the State of California, who over time sought my position and assistance. Superior Court Judge William Curtis, when he first planned to seek a politically elected office, to my amazement and surprise, knocked at the door of my humble East Salinas home. I didn't know him then; I thought he was a travelling salesman. He introduced himself as a practicing attorney from the Monterey Peninsula and that he intended to run for the office of district attorney for Monterey County. He requested an audience with me; he was so nice and humble, and showed no arrogance nor demonstrated any superior air, so I invited him into my parlor. I queried him on how he chose me, and he explained to me that a lot of people, Anglos and especially Pinoys (never mentioning names) had directed him to my open door.

We spent half a day together talking about issues, but mostly about law and order, crime and criminals, and about the injured public, the final losers of unlawful and illegal deeds. To make the story short, he ran for the coveted position, and I did everything possible within my capabilities to help in his campaign. He was elected and had been several times re-elected. His public service and his record as a DA and Public Defender were noteworthy, and he was later appointed Superior Court Judge for Monterey County. To the present day, when our roads crosses, he has never forgotten or ignored me, particularly when occasions required my consultation with the DA's office or when I needed enlightenment on legal matters. He has personally attended to me in the inner sanctum of his private office.

Another politician who knocked at my door of my Alisal Street home in Salinas is the incumbent state legislator representing our district, Rusty Areias, a bachelor and millionaire rancher from Los Banos, California. When he was "testing the waters" before officially throwing his hat into the political arena, he visited Salinas, accompanied by his sister. To be precise, he spent more than half a day with me at my humble abode. He did not precisely elucidate why he wanted to speak with me, but he was definite in saying that a lot of people introduced me to him indirectly, and hence he came over to visit. I had no inkling then, that he was a bachelor millionaire, and he never showed any sign that he was. He humbly introduced himself, explaining in minute detail the objects of his surprise visit. He asked me many questions about current issues. We discussed and exchanged opinions on numerous vital matters like agriculture and the farm workers, the needy and the indigents, veterans issues, problems relating to senior citizens, law and order, and many other human problems. His presentations appealed to my human understanding. We parted as friends and have been that way since. He ran for the office of state assembly, has been re-elected for a number of terms, and still remains a state assemblyman. He has not fully dimmed our relationship.[70]

Burt Talcott—a local lawyer who has represented our district in Washington for seven terms[71]—was on a constant wavelength with me during his incumbency. In most of his visits to his district to publicly report his views and activities in Washington, I was often given advanced notice of his visits, which I deemed as an invitation to be present at his public appearances. When the Marcos-Lopez Club of Monterey County[72] of celebrated their election in 1966, Representative Burt Talcott and his wife, upon my invitation as president of the club, flew from Washington, D.C. to grace our happy celebration. His address as our keynote speaker was enthusiastically received and applauded by all those in attendance. He was truly appreciative of how we conducted ourselves and honored us for not forgetting our roots and interests in our native homeland.

But to me personally, Talcott rendered me one of the highest accolades of my life. He did not only heartily listen intently to my concluding remarks, but he requested a copy of it. Of course, flattered by his unusual request, I gave him my only copy of the prepared remarks. For days, I wondered what our congressman would do with the worthless offerings of an unlearned peon like me. Not long after our now forgotten victory party, I received special delivery mail from the House of Representatives, Washington, D.C. Congressman Burt Talcott did not forget me; he again expressed his thanks for his opportunity to report and speak to his Filipino constituents, and he inserted in the envelope a copy of the Congressional Record which made me actually jump in joyous excitement. Talcott read and delivered my victory speech, unedited, to the assembled lawmakers in Congress—and without a word changed. A great honor indeed!

◆ ◆ ◆

One of the most rewarding campaigns I, many times, participated in was the Cal-Vet Home Loan Program in the State of California. This program was offered by the State of California for the benefit of California Veterans as part of a thank you reward to and for those who fought for freedom and democracy. Other states offered cash bonuses to the veterans in their state. California, on the other side of the coin, offered the Cal-Vet Program. The State of California sold bonds which were previously voted on and approved by the citizens and loaned the proceeds to needy and eligible California veterans at very low interest rates, primarily to purchase homes for their families.

This program, from its beginning to the present, had the total blessings of the American Legion and other veterans' organizations. As a Post Commander, District Commander, and Area Commander (Vice-Commander for the whole Department of California) of the American Legion, it was incumbent upon me—and it became my responsibility—to see that this program was perpetuated.[73] I have and will continue to do my utmost to see that bond elections for the Cal-Vet Home Loan Program continues. Every time the finances face extinction, we go to the citizens for permission to sell more bonds, and so far, the citizens have not failed California veterans. Unlike other programs, the Cal-Vet Program does not spend or use tax revenues. It is a self-supporting program that benefits the whole state of California. The government manages and administers this program through its appropriate and appointed agencies; they are responsible for the proper management, operation, and protection from financial embarrassments. Interest rates for this home loan program are far below those available on the open market.

My first home in Salinas, like many other Filipinos, was purchased through the Cal-Vet Program. Interest rates were then 3% below those available from banks and other financial institutions. And like other Cal-Vet homeowners, compared to the public financed homes, our monthly installments were far easier on the pocketbook for a California veteran. Another distinct feature of this program is that if the veteran failed to take advantage of it for any reasons, his/her wife or husband would become eligible to participate in the program. Reports and statistics show that there were just a few participants who failed to live up to their contract.

There was another campaign, County of Monterey-wise, that I took pleasure in participating. The Salinas Valley, known nationally as the "Salad Bowl of the Nation," is dependent upon the supply of precious fresh water. The valley, therefore, is characteristically jotted with thousands of water wells, not only for the vegetable crops we grow to feed the country, but also for home consumption by the populace. I labored in the fields as an irrigator so I had experienced cases especially when rainfall fell short of average, that some water pumps would run short of liquid gold, at times, spewing sand. To raise crops, farmers and growers were forced to dig deeper wells.

To relieve the county of digging and digging deeper wells, a campaign was instituted to build a dam in the southern portion of the county where rainwater could be stored and used to replenish the wells and the underground Salinas River during drought years. To finance this gigantic project, bonds were to be sold and be repaid by the residents of the water district through the increase of property taxes. But people were so deeply burdened by taxes, the very hated and unpopular means of raising money by the government and its agencies, that this project was not expected to receive popular approval. The plan was therefore presented to the people. Vigorous and strong campaigning was instituted to buck the seeming reluctance of the citizens to pay higher taxes, especially the property owners. I, as a property owner, was at first averse to paying more taxes, but after much deliberation and listening to the pros and cons, the advantages and disadvantages, ignored my self-interest and joined the forces whose minds were for the good of the whole valley.

It was an uphill battle for the Dam Bakers, but in the end we triumphed at the polls. Nacimiento Dam was constructed; the whole valley rejoiced in its benefits, and higher taxes were absorbed without complaint. Nacimiento Dam became a blessing to the valley and its citizens; it furnished not only the needed water to the valley; it became a highly regarded facility not only to outdoor enthusiasts but also to boaters, campers, anglers and fishermen. It is a much thought-of recreation area in the South County.

The Nacimiento Dam was built and appreciated but time soon proved its inadequacy. San Vicente Dam in proximity to

Nacimiento was soon built to augment and supplement the functions of the former. Now that it was discovered that salt water was seeping into the fresh water supply of our county, a phenomena that threatened the health and welfare of the people and the vegetable industry, the county is now seeking other options to save our lands from inevitable destruction.

◆ ◆ ◆

The City of Salinas, the largest incorporated entity in Monterey County, had always looked down on its suburb, East Salinas, once generally known maliciously as "Okie Town." The two areas were literally separated by railroad tracks. "Okie Town" was the place where the "Okies" and "Arkies" settled when they arrived here from the drought areas of Oklahoma, Arkansas, and Nebraska in the early 1930s (reminiscent of John Steinbeck's The Grapes of Wrath).[74] These people were never fully welcomed and accepted by the Salinas natives, the people that dictated the who, what, where, when, and why for the city and neighboring areas. These new immigrants, who came here in heavily laden, dilapidated cars—their entire wealth may be their total load—settled down in the East Salinas area, the Alisal District. They lived in tents, lean-tos, barns, or whatever shelter they could manage. They came, conquered, and established homes in this other-side-of-the-track dominion.

They were not initially loved and admired by the Salinas natives, but the farmers, growers, and shippers loved them as workers and laborers. They were migrant workers who worked hard, and some of them were able to acquire and maintain their residences in the Alisal area. Some of them, by hard work, thrift, and good planning, prospered. And in time, their economic status brightened. They brought families, relatives, and neighbors from their drought covered homes to California and the Alisal District. With the addition of minority groups, the Spanish, Asians, and other groups settling in East Salinas, the area soon grew to the extent of becoming as big as the original City of

Salinas.

As the Alisal township grew and threatened Salinas in size, people were thinking about incorporation, an idea springing greatly from the need for police protection, representation, and an actual voice in the control of their human existence. This movement in the Alisal neighborhood opened the eyes of the residents of the City of Salinas. They could not heartily relish the concept of a growing competing city situated across the railroad tracks. The idea of annexation was soon developed to curtail the thought of incorporation. The incorporation group, which had the backing of the pioneers of Alisal and the annexation factions of the region, had explorative studies of their positions. Both contrasting ideologists argued the advantages and disadvantages of their positions. It soon became evident that annexation would be the most ideal alternative, but the best solution was to allow the residents to make the final decision. Therefore, an election was scheduled to see what the citizenry actually wanted.

During these critical years, I had maintained a home in the Alisal District. We were not controlled politically by the City of Salinas; we fell under the jurisdiction of the County of Monterey. Alisal was a rural territory which was not politically and strictly controlled like an incorporated city. As Alisal residents, we built buildings, homes, and other structures without adhering to strict local regulations. We were allowed, without restriction, to do most of what we wanted with our property. Living outside city regulations, I opened up an office at my humble home, converting my garage into a business center. A license or a permit was not necessary. The County of Monterey did not then impose or require a license to transact business within its jurisdiction. If Alisal chose to incorporate, it was obvious that businesses within its jurisdiction would be taxed and levied assessments.

The annexation was approved by the residents and Alisal became part and parcel of the City of Salinas. I did dread the idea that I would be forcibly compelled to close shop, for I knew there was an existing city ordinance prohibiting businesses and offices in a residential district. I would then have to open an office in the city's business district which would mean bigger overhead and regular business hours. That idea would not equate with my part-time business. It would essentially cancel my part-time means of livelihood.

Either way the ball bounced—incorporation or annexation—my situation needed changes. During the heat of the campaign, I was caught in a very shaky, unsteady position. My heart and mind were inclined to work for annexation; they were favoring the building and growth of a city which would be the biggest between San Jose and Santa Barbara. However, my financial needs compelled me to favor incorporation, with the thought that I would be able to continue doing business with an office at the convenience of my humble home. But what was good for the community overpowered my personal needs. So I decided to seek the joining together of the two areas—Salinas and Alisal.

As the campaign progressed, I had the pleasure of meeting the mayor, who was in favor of annexation. It should be noted that his excellency and I were not total strangers. We had previously met and had many encounters. When he asked me if I was for or against the campaign, I frankly told him I was inclined to vote positively for the issue, but I explained to him that taking a positive position was hard for me to swallow; that by favoring annexation, I was cutting my own throat. I digressed at length at my predicament—that if Alisal became an integral part of Salinas, my business office, which was part of my home located in the residential neighborhood, may not conform with existing city ordinances. After listening to my presentation, he directly queried, "How long have you operated your office at your home?"

I told him I operated my small business there from the time I purchased the property in 1953. As an afterthought, he advised me to visit City Hall and explain to them my predicament. I listened to and followed his sage advice, went to the City Hall, and went home with a permit and license to continue doing business as usual in the privacy of my home. This new development gave me the proper incentive to campaign ardently and vigorously for the annexation. The suburb of Alisal, the previously demeaned "Okie Town," became by mandate of the people an integral part of the City of Salinas. Alisal then became an integral part of Salinas, enjoying all the joys and sorrows of a unified incorporated city.

◆ ◆ ◆

I attempted—by the inspiration of my colleague and good friend, Val Arellano, the first Filipino ever elected as a U. S. mayor,[75] and later Alex Alcantara, who also served as Councilman and Vice Mayor of Soledad, California,[76] as well as the urging by many friends and acquaintances—to run for public office. So in 1969, I filed for a seat for the City Council of Salinas, California.[77] There were two vacant positions in the City Council; there were seven of us contesting to fill these vacancies. Among us were two incumbents, both very popular and strong candidates. I ran on a platform that spoke for the benefits of the down-trodden, the forgotten, the ethnic population of the city. Housing and recreation were also my great concern. The campaign was divided into two separate ideologies: a business-minded city or a city embracing the whole spectrum of the city. The election resulted in the continuation of the former incumbents, who were retained as city councilors.

There was one incident during the campaign that I can't forget. Two of the candidates were running as a team. One day during the heat of the campaign, this couple invited me to meet with them to discuss strategy. All three of us agreed on some issues, especially regarding the lack of non-business people in the composition of city government and city commissions. At that period, all appointments to all the city commissions and committees came from the business community and/or their spouses. I agreed to meet with them. Their proposal was a shocking surprise. They, without reservation, bluntly requested me to quit the campaign and throw my undivided support to them. This action by my opponents sprung from the similarity of our campaign issues; we mutually favored some of the issues and followed the same courses of action. Since they were working as a team, they argued, it would make it more expeditious to achieve positive results. I suggested also that since we agreed on many of the issues, let me be a part of the team—let one of you withdraw. My proposition, of course, definitely fell on deaf ears.

In retrospect, I should have told them to jump in a lake. However, I tactfully told them that I was in the race to win. Win, lose or draw, I told them I would continue my campaign. I also had my pride; I didn't want to disappoint all the people that were working for my election. I did lose the election, but I did gain a lot of friends and admirers. I was urged to seek office at the election two years later. Even the retiring city mayor promised me his support if I decide to re-toss my hat in the ring. However, no amount of pressure could convince me to seek political office again!

Subsequent to this, other Filipinos in Salinas did emulate my aspiration to be a city councilman; they, too, got nothing but thumbs down by the voters. One problem these other candidates had was and is the fact that they had no exposure as a public volunteer to government agencies, commissions, or committees.

In 1972, the incumbent President, Richard M. Nixon, standard bearer of the Republican Party, was opposed by Senator George McGovern, the Democratic presidential nominee. I was then serving my second term as a member of the Democratic Central Committee of Monterey County. All components of the Central Committee were pledged to work wholeheartedly for the party and loyally campaign to preserve its platform and to support the election of all the chosen candidates. One month before that year's election, it became increasingly apparent to me that I could not positively, heartily and vigorously adhere to my pledge. As the campaign progressed, my dissatisfaction for Senator McGovern intensified to the point that I was prompted to resign my position so that I could be free to follow my heart's inclination. So, I handed in my resignation to our chairman, who was understandably dumbfounded. He had no recourse whatsoever to refuse my desire. In my resignation, I pointed out that "I could not vigorously campaign for the election of all the candidates running under the banner of the Democratic Party as it is presently organized." I, however, pledged and vowed to remain a member of the Democratic Party. Today, I am still a registered democrat and work for the election of many democratic aspirants of elective office.

I followed the campaign trails of Nixon and McGovern. Choosing between them, I decided that Nixon was the better man, stronger and wiser to lead the country. It should be noted here that I had never voted for "Dick" previously but putting the welfare of the nation over party affiliations, I felt Nixon would perform better. The actions of my fellow democrats toward me, however, made me completely lose faith. They censured me; they never hid their feelings of hatred for me and for my actions, which caused a rather explosive issue of the day. Their antagonism was greatly intensified by my re-election to the committee, a term to begin January 1 following the November elections. I did not, nor could I foresee the future. I guess nobody could surely see future events, for in the primary elections held in June before the presidential elections, I filed for and was elected for another two-year term as a member of the Democratic Central Committee of Monterey County.[78]

When the new panel of the Democratic Central Committee met in January, I could feel the antagonistic atmosphere that greeted me. But they did elect me, so there was no alternative for them but to accept me. Resolutions were presented to censure and to request—nay, demand—my resignation from the position. I took my place for a few months. There were members of the Democratic Party who urged me implicitly to serve my term as elected legitimately by the party, but in the course of time, I appeared to be a stumbling block for the Party to plow forward. Realizing that my presence caused disruptions in the meetings —and to let the Committee function collectively, efficiently, and effectively—I reluctantly vacated my seat.

I remained a democrat, and I continued to vote for and support democrats, but from that day forward, the Democratic Committee totally ignored me. To this day, I have no contact with of from the Democratic Party. The Republican Party, on the other hand, had adopted me to the extent that I am a regular recipient of most of their circulars, proposals, actions and other political papers. In fact, last year, 1994, they elected me a member of the Republican Party Platform Planning Committee, representing the 16th Congressional District, State of California.[79] This, I presume, is the irony of politics.

The Alisal School District was searching for school board members in 1984, when apparently mighty and complicated problems faced the district. This district is populated by a majority of Spanish-language speaking people, most of whom cannot communicate adequately in any other tongue. And in fact, many had little trust in non-Spanish speaking people. Therefore, their adherence to one another was strong. That did not mean, however, that they stuck together in all ways. They had their problems: family problems, peer problems, economic issues, and even politics. Most of the time, nevertheless, they would choose their kind when it came to leadership.

The majority of the teachers in the district, many of whom were non-Spanish speaking, were not completely satisfied with the way the district was managed. So, in their comprehensive search, they interviewed many applicants for would-be School Board candidates. They descended upon me and more or less pressured me to run for the school board position. If I did accept their proposition, they would do most of the campaigning and worked candidly for my election. I finally succumbed to their sincere urgings, but I intimated to them that we had a big mountain to climb. The final candidates composed of two Anglos, three Mexicans, one Filipino, and one Chinese person. I had many contacts with the Latino people in the Alisal area, and many of them had been clients in my small business venture.[80] But knowing them and doing business with them did not necessarily translate into getting their backing.

The campaign started with a bang. My campaign, however, suffered a large and immediate impediment. I was at that time serving as a member of the Monterey County Grand Jury[81] which was authorized to investigate all activities, governmental, political or any phase of activity within Monterey County. We could even investigate the judicial system if we wanted to or have sufficient reason to. I was specifically named a member of the Education Committee which focused its investigation of the Alisal School District. As a Grand Jury member, it was taboo for me to air publicly the results of our investigations.

I knew many of the problems of the Alisal District, yet my current situation forbade me to openly air them. I could have opened a pandora's box and contaminated the campaign with the dirt, but it would have compromised the sanctity of the Grand Jury. Our in-depth investigation revealed plenty of anomalies in the management of the district, especially in the disbursements of school funds. The superintendent and his cohorts under the open knowledge of the board members—their chairman, a local attorney and political activist—had appropriated school funds for personal expenditures. They—the superintendent and his cohorts—used school funds to vacation in Rome, used school cafeterias and supplies for the preparation of party feasts, and purchased with school funds vintage liquors for their parties. In fact, incumbent school officials were carrying school-sized checkbooks wherever they opted to go. There were many other anomalies too numerous to mention,[82] and the Monterey County Grand Jury final report lists these charges in detail. As a result, four of the school officials including the superintendent were incarcerated, confined in disgrace to atone their mistakes.

Going back to the school board campaign: At the peak of the campaign, I experienced many discriminatory actions. First, many of my posters staked in front yards would mysteriously disappear. In some cases, we would replace the placards, but they were never left alone. We nailed some posters on garage doors; if not torn to shreds, posters would be covered with graffiti.

One day, the three Mexican candidates made an appointment with me to meet them at the law offices of one of the candidates. They propositioned me to quit the race for the Alisal School District and shift my candidacy to the Salinas Union High School District. I, however, did not want to abandon the people who put their un-alienable trust on me, so I politely rejected their proposition. I stuck to the campaign against them. A week prior to the day the voters would be casting their precious votes, one of the local TV stations—one that prominently broadcast Spanish programs—interviewed all the candidates for airing. A camera crew came to my house, the interviewer asking questions with pen and notebook and the camera man focusing his machine on me. But although they informed me that all the interviews would be aired publicly before the election, the interview with me was not shown. Instead, they casually mentioned that Manuel L. Luz was another candidate. This action, discriminatory in every sense, was concocted by the Spanish clique. It infuriated the Anglo candidates; they told me in no uncertain terms that politics, dirty and cruel, was the way to cut down opposition.

Let me also point herewith, that a new superintendent was appointed to take the vacated position of the embezzling superintendent. A very capable school official currently employed by the district, a black educator, was ignored and bypassed, in order to hire a Latino educator to run our schools. The black superintendent was admired and respected by the teachers and principals in the Alisal area. But the clamor for a Latino educator was the only alternative acceptable, so the Latino population finally got their wish. This new superintendent was already performing his assigned duties during our campaign for the school board. So as a candidate for the school board of his district and as a resident of this area, I twice attempted to meet him at his office. I did believe that as a prospective board member, it would be a nice gesture to meet him and talk to him personally. But I was never given the opportunity to meet his acquaintance. I knew he was in his inner sanctum but the clerks in the front office, mostly Latino women, shut me out completely, even after notifying them I was running for the school board, a potential man to whom he would be answerable.

Needless for me to mention, I lost the election. And in some ways, I was grateful. Not long after the election, however, one vacancy occurred on the School Board, a position which must and could be filled by the board members by appointment and not necessarily by election. I was approached and asked if I still wanted to serve the School District. After carefully deliberating the offer, I modestly told them that my interests had waned and faded and that I had other important commitments to attend.

◆ ◆ ◆

In all the decades since I first settled in Salinas, I had always, in small doses, participated in State, County or City elections. In addition to the aforementioned activities, I had extended whatever I could within my capabilities in the campaigns and elections of such political leaders as: Alan Short (U.S. Senator), Robert Nimmo (California State Senator), Bob Wood (State Assemblyman), Carrol Hallet (State Assemblywoman), Arthur Atteridge (former Mayor of the City of Salinas and Monterey County Board of Supervisors),[83] and Barbara Shipnuck (Monterey County Board of Supervisors).[84] The popular Russ Jeffries, ex-mayor and councilman of the City of Salinas, was a very intimate and loyal friend of Salinas Valley Filipinos. He also received my endorsements and voluntary assistance in all his political campaigns.[85]

My appointment to the Traffic/Transportation Commission[86] came about in a very unusual but interesting way. At first, when he broached his interest in naming me to the Traffic/ Transportation Commission, I showed great reluctance. That weekend following his telling me of his intention, he appeared as a guest speaker at a Filipino Community of Salinas Valley social function. To my shocking surprise, he mentioned during his address his desire to name me to the Traffic and Transportation Commission. Then he asked the hundreds of Filipinos gracing the affair if they were willing to endorse his appointing me into the designated commission. A resounding endorsement by those present was a firm approval to his question. I served the Commission until his term of office was terminated.

"To sin by silence when they should protest makes cowards out of men." Ella Wheeler Wilcox

It was a little odd, the first time I ever read this chapter. My dad never ever told anyone in the family about any of the romantic involvements he had had prior to meeting Mom. And in a way, children never want to hear that. Children would rather believe that their parents came into being, fully formed and already betrothed. But life is more complicated than that.

As for the story of how our parents met, however, this was one we all knew. For they would tell bits and pieces of this embellished story at the dinner table, my mom and dad sometimes gleefully arguing about the nitpicky details of when and where and how and who. But it was a fun story, one that we regaled in as a family over the years.

Of course, the stories of their lives together are also the stories of our childhoods. Living life on 1805 East Alisal Street, having our mom take care of us in the mornings and our dad in the evenings, learning the value of money by watching our parent's penny-pinch and work extremely hard, even the story of their separation when I was seven—all of these stories and many more constitute the memories which make us who we are.

7. THE ROAD TO FAMILY CONTENTMENT

It was a little odd, the first time I ever read this chapter. My dad never ever told anyone in the family about any of the romantic involvements he had had prior to meeting Mom. And in a way, children never want to hear that. Children would rather believe that their parents came into being, fully formed and already betrothed. But life is more complicated than that.

As for the story of how our parents met, however, this was one we all knew. For they would tell bits and pieces of this embellished story at the dinner table, my mom and dad sometimes gleefully arguing about the nitpicky details of when and where and how and who. But it was a fun story, one that we regaled in as a family over the years.

Of course, the stories of their lives together are also the stories of our childhoods. Living life on 1805 East Alisal Street, having our mom take care of us in the mornings and our dad in the evenings, learning the value of money by watching our parent's penny-pinch and work extremely hard, even the story of their separation when I was seven —all of these stories and many more constitute the memories which make us who we are.

Marriage, an institution practiced and acknowledged throughout this universe, had always been alien to my personal participation. Not that I didn't agree with the concept of marriage or the value of family, but I placed myself separate from its implications. When I came to America, and temporarily severed relationships with my family, I felt that I had to, by sheer necessity, brave the unknown and live an existence based on my own untested direction. Whatever happened in my life, whatever touched me, I did alone. It was an alternative I chose, based primarily and considerably from what I saw, heard, and read about. So, I lived for many decades a confirmed bachelor, insulated from the magnetic attraction emanating from this institution.

As a young, debonair, penniless lad in the Philippines, I

was betrothed by my parents to Maria, a girl next door. Her family and mine agreed that we would make an ideal couple. And they never hid their pride about what they called a very perfect match. Many people who knew of the negotiated betrothal pact actually believed it may come to pass. The sad part of their deal, however, was that the girl next door and I were never consulted. She and I were great friends; we attended parties and dances together, and we enjoyed each other's company. But the essence of a relationship like marriage was not there. The other devastating effect was that it tended to drive away those men whose faces sparkled when they met the girl; and it also was a detriment for me to seek relationships with other young beauties.

There was a secondary "betrothal" which my school friends concocted. By word of mouth, they started the rumor that Marcelina, a particular charming beauty, and yours truly, were going steady. This rumor was believed as the gospel truth by many of our mutual friends and acquaintances. When the rumor reached us, she and I were both flabbergasted. We were simply schoolmates and close friends. However, she accused me of being the instigator of the big lie, and contrarywise, I was ready to point the finger at her. After a heart-to-heart talk, we agreed that we were both innocent. We also agreed to play the parts, to amuse those principal scheme mongers. And we thought we pulled the wool over the eyes of many of them. There was laughter in our hearts; there were deceiving smiles on the outside. The mock engagement even reached an ardent admirer of hers, who was then living in Portland, Oregon. After I had come to the US, I bumped into him while seeking employment in the fish canneries in Alaska. Assertively, he confronted me, demanding to know the truth of our relationship. I assured him that the coast was clear, and that if he really loved the girl, to not falter or slow his pursuit. Since leaving home, I never had any connection in any manner or form with "my betrothed."

There was a beautiful girl, Amalia, a dream girl, an intimate friend of one of my sisters, who I thought had a "crush" on me. And truth be told, I was also attracted to her gracious beauty.

Almost every day, she stopped at our bamboo-nipa hut to pick up, as she declared, my sister to attend school. We often talked, chatted, and laughed together as she awaited my sister. I sensed an attraction, a magnet pulling us closer; however, the attraction lacked the space and time to develop into a definite relationship. At the time, I was planning to seek greener pastures in the USA, an absence based upon statistics supplied by townmates who were then in the US for no more than five years. When she became aware of my plans, she showed great disappointment, but bravely received the news, offering me her prayers and wishing me good luck in my imminent venture. However, she made me promise not to forget her and to write her letters as often as time permitted. She also promised to answer all and every letter she would receive. The pledge of writing one another was the only definite and meaningful understanding or commitment between the two of us.

The promise of corresponding with her, I kept diligently for almost a year. My tired body, due to the physical demands of my work, became a mass of steel, as adrenalin revved up the heart when I poured my feelings and soul into my regular twice-a-month letters to her. But she failed to write me the anticipated answers, and never did I hear from her. I then purposed to pour my heart into my work instead. So as time flew—that was almost a year—the spark of electricity slowly but surely dimmed. By then, I had accepted the fact that she did not have an iota of care and love for me and to further pursue the hunt was futile.

Not many moons passed after I stopped the letters, I received a perfumed, studded-with-kisses letter from the Philippines. The missive demanded why I reneged on my vow to pen her. I sent back a letter of explanation that described the many unanswered letters I mailed her, that I kept my promise as a gentleman and a scholar, and that I only stopped when I didn't hear from her. It must have been a shock to her when she confronted her parents regarding where the letters went. She was apologetic on her following letter, relating that her parents decided to extradite her to Manila to pursue a higher education after I left and that my letters were denied her possession. Her parents took possession of my letters with no intention of sharing them with her, making "bonfires" of them as they classified them as trash, decidedly to cut off any further communication between the two of us. She wrote me a very long letter—a newspaper—detailing the facts, and asking forgiveness not only for the unanswered letters, but also on the uppity behavior of her parents. She reiterated her desire to renew communications between us.

The true picture was based, in my estimation, on the strata of society prevalent in the Philippines before and now. Her family was middle class—socially, financially, and politically. In other words, they belong to the elite. They had no desire nor intention to dilute their status by admitting onto their pedestal, a peon, struggling beggar like me. Such was the custom in the homeland in those days, and in most cases, is still prevalent today. The country mouse can never mix with the city dudes. Having been reminded of my indigent roots, having been given the lesson never to enter into the portals of the elite, even by invitation, I learned to gracefully accept my honest lot. I decided without reservation to completely sever any and all connections with her and her family.

Many, many years later, it came to pass that, at one of my rare visits to the old haunts in the city of my birth, my sister and I decided to visit the market place. As my sister and I alighted from a *kalesa*[87] at the entrance of the mall, a lady who was about to board another *kalesa*, recognized me and shouted my name, "Maning, when did you come back from the States?"

When my name was called, I looked around to see if there might be another Maning nearby. There was not another male around, so I was positive I was the person being addressed. I then approached her, answering in my most polite behavior all the questions she opted to ask. Finally, as she satisfied her inquisitiveness, she boarded her *kalesa* with the parting invitation, "Come visit us at the house—we are still in the same location. Come anytime. There will always be open-door welcome for you."

I acknowledged her kind invitation and promised to visit her as time permitted.

When she finally drove off, I asked my sister, who courteously kept her distance from our seemingly cordial meeting and conversation, "Who is that lady I was talking with?"

"Manong," she said, "Please stop pulling my leg. The way you behaved and conducted yourself, and the manner you acted before her, made me believe without doubt that you knew who she was."

I confessed to my sister that I positively had no inkling as to the identity of the mysterious lady. I acted as I did to give her the benefit of the doubt and show her that I was a gentleman, and not a pretender and a snob from abroad. When she finally identified the lady in the *kalesa*, I almost fainted. She was my "dream girl," the lady whose parents denied her my feelings and possibly a permanent commitment. I never intended to keep my promise to visit her—my dream girl had turned into a nightmare!

◆ ◆ ◆

I have personally known the numerous family problems of many friends, acquaintances, and countrymen. I have been an advocate, counselor, and public relations officer for many families facing marital or family problems. I was privy to the status of children involved in these situations. My familiar and personal knowledge of these perplexed family problems strengthened my loathing to become a family man. Some of my married friends used to brand me selfish or antisocial because I stayed a die-hard bachelor. It was not—I repeat—that I abhorred the institution of marriage, nor did I object to others entering blissful matrimony. The main factor that I feared was the fate of my offspring if I became a family man. I feared and hated the thought that I might fail to adequately give them the comfort and education that they deserved.

I have seen, with my own eyes, situations where children lacked sufficient nourishment or were improperly dressed to equalize the inclement weather. Abused children, single-parent children, abandoned children, illiterate and unhealthy offspring were not alien to me. Those situations were what I failed to accept and feared if I succumbed to the institution of marriage.

Many of my friends and acquaintances continued to abet, encourage, or rib me toward the institution of marriage. They wanted to see me lose my bachelorhood. Therefore, they tried to acquaint me with relatives—nieces, sisters, and even neighbors living in the Philippines. They gave me names, addresses, and letters of introduction. There were so many that I would not have sufficient time to correspond with all of them. Truly, I corresponded with a number, some employed, others mostly students.[88]

One particularly young beauty, May, to whom I was introduced, belonged to a good family in the Ilocos. I was introduced to her by her cousin, a friend who lived in Salinas. We exchanged letters which were cordial and informational at the beginning but as time elapsed, they became more and more intimate, and there came to pass a considered long-distance understanding. Suddenly, her letters included a scheme which she described as a business venture that may be profitable to our future. She told me that she was going into the "buy and sell business," a profitable endeavor, she claimed. She suggested that I send her merchandise which she would market at home. I shipped a few items she requested, but her subsequent orders became more bulky and costly, and I found myself in a quandary. I window-shopped for her orders, but prior to purchasing the goods, I decided to let her cousin peruse the letter. She was shocked by the orders—she seemed to smell a rat, a scum. She advised me to keep the merchandise on hold while she investigated what was brewing in her cousin's mind. The letter she received in reply made her so humiliated that she could barely face me. She was so humbled in shame that there were actual tears in her eyes. Her informers back home reported that my correspondent was recently married, and that I was being made the goat of a scheme that was profitable to the newlyweds! From this situation, I learned a lesson never to get involved in a tele-correspondence relationship again.

The year 1954 was a year which is quite memorable to me. In this year, I decided to acquire me a nest, a home of my own, a haven where I could do things freely and independently. At the same time, I also acquired interest on another house in North Salinas. This was made possible in part because I had landed a position as a correctional officer with the State of California, Department of Corrections.[89] A confirmed bachelor, a steady and permanent means of livelihood, and a "pad" at my discretion—what a life![90]

Now that I was comfortably settled in my humble home, the offers for introductions to relatives—young females of course—multiplied tremendously. My lesson learned made me skeptical of their offers no matter how tempting they were. My house also became a beehive of activities during weekends, especially during school breaks. I gained the friendships of many young coeds from home, all of them taking post-graduate studies at UC Berkeley and other colleges in the San Francisco Bay area. With the offer of a party, they would descend upon my home in droves, sometimes two or three carloads full with the drivers being the only men in the group. There, they craved the succulent *lechon*, the main dish during these parties. These excursions were not however spur of the moment occurrences. I had built a barbecue pit and lechon range in my backyard, and an open patio adjacent to the cooking pits, and supplied the necessities, but these coeds did all the laborious culinary chores. And I would be forewarned days ahead so that the hog was ready when they arrived.

With all these young, intelligent, charming coeds becoming my weekend guests, I, as a bachelor, had the opportunity to pick the prize of the pack. Fancy, free and matured, I could not single out anyone. I loved them all, each and every one of them. There must have been something in my nature that prevented me from separating one from the group. Eventually many of these young women, having completed their missions in this country, would return back to the homeland to impart unto the folks the knowledge acquired in America. Now I wonder if I did single out one of them, would she had consented? I wonder, wonder!

◆ ◆ ◆

In 1959, when some of my married contemporaries were singing lullabies to grandchildren, a tornado-force soothing wind visited my serene home and forced an about-face in my life. The friend who introduced me to her "buy and sell" entrepreneurial cousin in the Philippines had not stopped trying to find me a mate. But this time, it was not one of those far-flung, correspondence romances. This particular subject was already strolling the paved jungles of America.

My friend, Elena, and her husband, Delfin Cruz, a newspaper publisher, had travelled to Chicago, Illinois, to visit relatives and friends. There, they learned of the plight of the younger sister of a close friend. Cresencia Aranilla was completing her two-year contract as an exchange nurse and was required to return to the Philippines soon. She had learned that there was an impossible chance to extend her student nurse visa through the Immigration Naturalization Service Office (INS) in Chicago. Delfin and Elena were able to convince Cresencia to come to Salinas with them for a visit and they assured her that she could get an extension of her legal residency at the San Francisco INS—through me.

Delfin was well aware of my successes in solving many immigration problems for Filipinos,[91] so his assurance to Cresencia of a beneficial solution to her problem depended on my able assistance. Therefore, he informed me by mail ahead of time of their return to Salinas and detailed the ramifications of her problem so that I could be prepared for the emergency. Time complicated the matter.

Editha, the daughter of my brother Lucas, had obtained her visa to America and I anticipated my niece landing on US soil soon. In preparation for her arrival, I added another bedroom, a separate dining area, and a laundry room to my small two-bedroom chalet. The construction was near completion, so I had invited a few close friends to celebrate the additional structure. A couple of days prior to the celebration party, the Cruz family returned to Salinas with their guest. They were then added to the party invitees.

The morning of the party, Delfin, Elena, and Cres went sightseeing in and around Salinas, a detour planned before they landed at my doorstep that evening. Cres was filled with surprise as she had exclaimed, "This is not the house I slept in last night." After introductions were made, the party continued. With barbecued chicken and steaks, as well as the comradeship and the laughter, Cres took notice. Above all, she noticed the appreciable closeness of the Filipinos in Salinas, a relationship unknown in Chicago or in any of the cities on the Atlantic Coast.

When everyone had enjoyed the feast, Elena and Cres volunteered to wash the dishes. As the two busied about their tasks, Elena began to share with Cres what she knew about my life. What struck Cres was that I was a bachelor living alone in my own house working steadily at a reputable job. As I was entered the kitchen, I overheard her disbelief of my single status. Astonished, she asked Elena, "You talk about him being a bachelor, yet I see laundry hanging on the *sampayan*.[92] Who does all the washing?"

Without giving Elena a chance to answer, I retorted, "It was Manuela, who does all my laundry." That confused our visitor, who then demanded to know who Manuela was. Elana, who was grinning from amusement, then explained that Manuela and Manuel were the same person, and that I referred to "Manuela" whenever I did chores normally performed by women.

The days following the party were days of planning and preparing the necessary documents to convince the INS that our visitor from the Windy City deserved an extension of her stay in the United States. In doing so, I spent hours with Cres, preparing her for the coming inquisition which was to follow. Two days elapsed, then I drove her and her hosts to San Francisco to file the application for extension with the essential backup documents. Although we didn't get a decision right away, we were told that a decision would be forthcoming within the week.

We came back to Salinas with the visitor fearfully anticipating a rejection. I kept reassuring her not to be pessimistic about her request, but to be remain optimistic and have hope. Within ten days, she was totally jubilant. The response to her extension request gave her an extra six months to wind up and enjoy her stay.

Meanwhile, the home of the Cruz's was every day infested by would-be Romeos and Lotharios when it was graced by the presence of the fair lady from Chicago. She had the pre-emption to select any one of them—or should I say, any one of *us*. I passed away my spare time at the Cruz home, primarily because I wanted to know the outcome of my efforts and secondarily, to acquiesce to their insistent invitations. Maybe, perhaps maybe, the lady also wanted to show her appreciation and gratitude for my help. As the days passed, we began to be together more often, as she became more distant from the others.

We began to know each other more intimately as she related to me her past life, the joys and unhappiness she went through. In return, I confided to her some of the ups and downs of my unworthy existence. As these stories unfolded, as our association became closer, we commenced looking at the lonely man in the moon. Something beyond elucidation was happening to me. My steadfastly insulated heart was melting. The confirmed bachelor was losing his vows for the single existence. Was I in love and was that love taking all of me? Was she experiencing a similar transformation? Then one night—under a full moon and with the lonely man residing in it as a witness—something like a bolt of lightning struck the both of us. We agree that we were one—two lives melted and merged as an entity. We were in love; we became engaged. The vows and defenses I deliberately built for over a half century crumbled like melted pillars of ice.

Before our mutual agreement and our meeting of the minds, she proposed that the relationship should be on a 50/50 basis. Frankly, I adamantly rejected her idea. She asked me why and what did I want. I told her that it would be more agreeable with me if we were 51/49 with me getting the greater advantage. I told her that I wore the pants and in marriage, I wanted to hold that advantage.[93] A pro and con discussion made her surrender to my position.

She had to go back to Chicago to wind up her business and to gather her worldly possessions. But prior to her returning there, we had already planned to put a seal to our commitment. Upon her return to Salinas, we planned to elope to the Biggest Little City (Reno) to consummate our life commitment.

Absence, it is universally claimed, makes the heart grow fonder. Cresencia proved the literal truth of this adage. She burned the wires connecting our distant locations.[94] It got to the point that after a week of her absence, I was infuriated, beyond comprehension, by a call from the local telephone company. In a serene, pleasant voice, the telephone representative posed to me this question: "Mr. Luz, when will you settle your telephone bill? We noticed that your account is skyrocketing rapidly, and we request you to make ready arrangements for a settlement."

Shocked by the demand, I responded, "Lady, how can I pay my account when you have not yet posted the bill? Please mail me the bill and without hesitation, I will immediately transmit you my check. Is that not the proper and appropriate way business is transacted?" The problem was settled immediately without any more question.

Delfin, Elena, and I met Cres at the San Francisco Airport upon her return from the Windy City. When she entered the terminal, I played possum as the Cruz's welcomed her. She showed great disappointment when they told her I was called for urgent duty, and that to my deepest regret, I could not forsake my employment, but would be waiting with open arms and affection when we met in Salinas. I tailed them towards the baggage carousel, making sure that she would not notice me. As she picked up her baggage, I suddenly and sneakily appeared beside her saying, "Can I help you with your baggage, Madam?" Her surprise was real astonishment, but she accepted our ploy with the biggest smile and a leaping, joyous heart.

The day following her joyous return, we trekked to Nevada, or more specifically to Reno, to legalize our commitment. However, things work out in mysterious ways at times. Instead of taking the more direct route to Reno, we re-routed, without much thought through Lake Tahoe south shore, where we enjoyed dinner and a couple of hours wrestling with the one-armed bandits. After depositing a few unlucky dollars, we continued to Reno, our intended destination. The night was not getting young, and tired and sleepy, we decided to spend the night in Carson City. The next morning, while partaking in the motel's free coffee and breakfast, the server happened to inquire where we were heading. Delfin, our intended witness, readily responded, "Our destination is Reno, and this couple intends to pronounce the sacred 'I do's' there."

"Why do you have to go to Reno?" commented the man behind the counter. "City hall is just across the street, and marriages are solemnized there every day. It will be open for business at eight."

Reno was immediately shelved. At opening time, we were the first in line before the presiding judge. There was some unintended delay, however, in the ceremony. When the magistrate asked for the rings, we could not produce them pronto. In our eagerness and excitement, my bride had them locked in her night bag, which was stored in the car trunk parked across the street. I had to hurriedly go fetch them, causing the delay, and I had to ransack the contents of the bag to have and to hold the missing links. Gasping with embarrassment, with the forgotten rings in my grasp, the ceremony was solemnized and our dream to live, cherish, and obey one another became a reality. After the wedding, Cresencia Aranilla Luz and I proceeded to Reno to spend the weekend![95]

We settled down into our humble chalet, content that we had a roof over our heads and, though it was simply furnished, not elaborate like other homes. My new bride accepted the condition without complaint. I could not schedule a vacation from my job as a correctional officer,[96] so I had to go "back to the pits." Cres intently watched me prepare my lunch, and I also informed her of my duty hours.[97] So she was left alone, with all the time at her disposal. But her paramount concern as she confessed was my welfare. Knowing the contents of my lunch box—a sandwich, a cookie, fruit, and coffee—she assumed that I would be famished when I got home. So, she attempted to prepare a hot meal, ready to be served at 2:30 p.m., my usual arrival time. I appreciated her concern and her efforts; however, there was an apparent flaw in her intentions. She simply did not have the know-how to prepare the rice as we Asians commonly do.

When I came home from work and parked the car in the carport, the aroma of burnt rice filled the air. I found her in tears, hurt by her due mistakes, apologizing. Cres confessed that she tried to cook three pots of rice, but they all turned out uncomplimentarily. Secretly amused by her confession,[98] I demonstrated to her the magic of preparing the staple food. She was a good student; she repeated the chore that evening, meticulously following my instructions and everything turned out excellently. In jest, I told her how pleased I was that she treated me like a Greek god, giving me burnt offerings. Now, she dismisses it with a sneer and smile.[99]

The lack of culinary expertise which my wife demonstrated at her first attempt inspired her to improve her skills. There were many invitations to family dinners that we received and attended, and in every one of these outings, she would pester the host for recipes of the dishes served. She would then beg me to buy the needed ingredients. She would cook them, and I became "the guinea pig." This practice became a bit of an obsession; she practiced and practiced, and with my ever-ready assistance, she has become quite an adept as a cook.

Our trip to Nevada was not known by any soul save for the Cruz clan, who after our return, could not refrain from making it public. As a newspaper man, Delfin not only aired it in his publication, The Philippines Mail,[100][101] but also with the local daily publications. These tidings surprised everyone who knew me. Our home phone kept ringing all day, even nights, from surprised friends offering us their salutatory congratulations. My new bride was overwhelmed by the many congratulations, some of whom were accompanied by invitations to dinner. As may be expected, however, she also received some uncomplimentary jealousy-tainted messages, which I advised her to forget. She, naturally, was inflicted with pain by these unfavorable remarks; she finally, upon my advice and requests, learned to treat them with a grain of salt.

One of my best friends in Salinas was Paulina Morales, a respected Filipina lady. Our paths converged in this locality. We started as friendly adversaries advocating different views on many issues. Her husband was a labor contractor. I advocated unionization of the workers. As I mellowed my labor activities and as she learned more about me, we smoked the "peace pipe" and buried the hatchet. The focus of our meeting of the minds arose from her close relationship with one of my sisters in the Philippines. When she found out that Salvacion was one of my sisters, she embraced me like a long-lost brother. It came to light that she and my sister were like bosom-sisters during their student days, even sharing their belongings and clothes with each other. Consequently, she accepted me as an adopted brother.

A reception party for our wedding was prepared by my "sister" after she learned about our elopement. She invited many friends but mostly the so-called "elites" of the Filipino community to a surprise elaborate feast for me and my bride, graced by the leaders of our Filipino society. My new bride was amazed at what was happening, but the most notable thing was that she was introduced to many of my friends and to our community leaders. It was a very happy, gala occasion—with just one minor sour note. Most of the couples attending made remarks that since the groom was an old bachelor, way passed a half century young, it would be next to impossible for me to sire an heir or heiress. Those predictions were uncalled for, but we, the bride and groom, merely smiled away their pessimisms.

These friends, the pessimists and the predictors, were surprised and even shocked when time proved them wrong. Within three years of marriage, I successfully sired two hale and healthy sons, Manuel Junior and Marcel. But the most surprised and probably jealously hurt were those younger, married couples who plunged into the matrimonial pool ahead of me. Well, mother nature has a way of treating her children in a million different ways.

When Cres left the Philippines, she carried with her a heavy burden in her heart. She was fighting for the sole custody of her two sons from a previous marriage, and she had left her sons in the Philippines under her sister's care when she came to the USA. After our marriage, she intensified her efforts by engaging the services of two Filipino lawyers, who after three years of legal maneuvers, succeeded in getting the Philippine courts to decide in favor of maternal custody. Within a week after she was judged the custodial parent, the two boys, Rhubardo and Godofredo,[102] enplaned to the United States to live with their loving mother. We became a family of six in 1964. It was a hard-fought litigation which also cost plenty. Most of her earnings[103] during the court battle went to legal fees; however, we felt that the ends justified the means. It was money well spent.

When both parents are engaged in pursuing their professions or avocations, children often suffer the most. This is actually the consequence if both work the same hours and the children are entrusted into the hands of a babysitter. Babysitting also absorbed a significant percentage of the parents hard-earned finances. To solve this posing dilemma, my wife and I devised a plan which we believed would solve the problem. It required and necessitated a great amount of sacrifice, but we pledged to adhere to the novel plan and we put it in operation.

The blueprint which we put into practice was that we staggered our working hours so that one of us would always be with our four sons any time of the day. I arranged with my employer, the Department of Corrections, to permanently schedule my working hours from 5:30 a.m. to 2:00 p.m. In turn, she worked the afternoon shift, 3:00 p.m. to 11:00 p.m., at Salinas Valley Memorial Hospital. She tended to the kids in the morning, and I took over when I came home at 2:30 p.m., just in time for her to go to work. It was a case of saying hello and goodbye to each other at the door. We worked this plan for many years.[104]

For my wife—who had experience in handling young children as well as babies at the hospital—this arrangement was a breeze. But to me, a mere novice, I had to learn a lot. Changing diapers, preparing formula, singing lullabies, knowing when to put them to bed—these practices were alien to me. However, my love for my children made me determined to meet the challenge; my outlook for their future inspired me to conquer all obstacles.

My family responsibilities were further complicated by my responsibilities to my clients in my small business. My home office, a converted garage, sometimes become a beehive of activity, especially in the evenings, for the majority of my clients were agricultural workers. I possessed licenses in real estate and insurance, as well as being a licensed tax preparer and a commissioned notary public. I also did consultations on immigration and naturalization and travel to the Philippines.[105] These chores complicated my obligations to my young sons, but sacrificially I am proud of it. I overcame them all satisfactorily.

◆ ◆ ◆

We were heartily enjoying the blessings of family life when a problem began to appear on the horizon. My wife was being pestered—on the phone and in personal contacts—with women who nettled her with the posing question, "Why don't you buy a more luxurious home? Both you and your husband are gainfully employed. Why are you tolerating spending your days in a dilapidated building? You deserve a beautiful home."

True, our house was not on par with their homes, in structure, appearance, and more so in value, and my wife realized these apparent differences. She then tried to get me agree to relocate to a new house. I did, however, adamantly refuse to accede to her desires. The pressures from her so-called friends continued to every day reach her. Finally, by 1967, she could no longer bear the increasing influence of those unrelenting and overbearing callers.

Without me knowing, she began house hunting, and found one that attracted her liking. She then confronted me and forced me to look over the house. It was really a well-built structure, nicely surrounded by a well-groomed garden and back patio. Like my wife, I also would have liked to dwell in this house beautiful. Nevertheless, as I saw it, there were many disadvantages that deterred me from moving from our humble home. Know ye, that I am a simple man, fully satisfied with simple things. My adamant refusal to move to another location infuriated my wife. Undeterred, I informed her that even if we purchased the house of her choice, I would not uproot myself from my present abode.

She, in her anger and frustration, decided that the old house was not her home, and she sought residence in another neighborhood in the city. I was coming home from work one afternoon, to find a huge moving van parked regally in front of the house. It was loaded with almost all the home furnishings. She told me that she and the children—our own two sons and her two from her previous marriage—were moving out. And she confronted me with a challenging question, "Are you coming with us?"[106]

What was happening struck me surprisingly. I was stunned by this unexpected turn of events. She had positively determined to move, and it would be impossible to stop her. Finally, I decided, "I am staying here. I am sorry I cannot agree to go where you opt to settle."[107]

The boys also hated moving to a new neighborhood, with no friends and a new school, but they had to be with their mother. They moved to a house in the neighborhood near Hartnell College.[108] I opted to dwell simply in my "unfurnished East Salinas house."

During our separation, which stemmed from our different attitudes and contradicting real estate opinions, we met several times to negotiate a clear settlement. She persisted on the desire to purchase a new home, just as persistently as she was being pressed by her friends. She claimed that she earned enough to pay the obligations and responsibilities for acquiring the new home. And she cited examples of other Filipinas whose paychecks were less than ours. I countered that we surely may be able to afford the luxury of a new home, but if we followed our desires without knowing all the facts, we may, like others, fall prey to unwanted predicaments.

My little knowledge in real estate finally crumbled her arguments. I pointed out to her that if we purchased a home on installment for thirty years, the total cost of the property would amount to perhaps three times the cost of the original purchase. In other words, her monthly payment would not apply fully to the loan—and most of it would be absorbed by interest. The amortization process baffled her. I pointed out to her, in addition, that she may be exceedingly surprised to find out that many families living in beautiful houses with new cars parked in their driveways, may have their cupboards and refrigerators bare to the bone.[109] Finally, I told her, even if I consented to buy her another house, I would not join her in dwelling in it. I also pointed to her some financial setbacks we would encounter. For example, once we moved out into a new location, my home office would have to be closed and could not be transferred to a residential area. To continue serving my clientele, I would have to rent, at added expense, an office in the business district. I also reminded her that at our present location, farm products—all kinds of vegetables, onions, garlic, and even fruit—were dropped at our doorstep by clients and friends, which decreased our grocery bills considerably. Finally, I declared to her and in the presence of the children, "Which one would you prefer—and I want you to think deeply and intelligently on this—a car in the garage or chicken on the table? No turning back and no regrets."

In the end, she opted for the chicken on the table. And so, at the end of the school year, they moved back home. The children were happy and delighted to come home, back to friends and a school they were accustomed to.[110] Luckily, they didn't sign a lease on the house they moved into. They only paid rent for a month so they had a roof over their heads for that duration. While they were gone, and the house being practically bare, I took advantage of the situation by putting some improvements in. The home face-lifting completed, the entire family lived united at the old residence.

After everything settled back to normalcy, Cres and I spent time to plan our financial program. Firstly, we decided that the would-be babysitting fees be set aside and placed in savings for the children's future. We also agreed that all household expenses would come from my earnings and that her income would be saved exclusively for our future and for unforeseen family expenditures. We also agreed to use our credit cards in moderation. We felt cash transactions were fruitful and advantageous so ultimately, we made purchases by cash or in three-month contracts sans interest, otherwise we would have to temporarily go without. This financial planning continued to the day we were both retired (or as we say, "retarded").

Most families are accustomed to granting weekly allowances to their offspring beginning at grade school age. We opted not to adopt this popular practice. A novel idea was conceived which we felt would teach the children the real value of money. We placed a cigar box full of change (of course, we knew the amount)—nickels, dimes, quarters, and half dollars—in a drawer with a pad of paper and a pencil. We directed the boys to draw whatever amount they need at school, write the amount drawn on a sheet of paper, and signed it. At the end of the week, we would get together to audit their necessary expenditures. If one of them proved to be extravagant, the rest would jump on the culprit and demand an explanation. The boys, therefore, learned thriftiness and the value of their assets.

One of them, however, was slick and tricky, and we caught him taking money and signing not his name but any of his brothers'. Eventually this stepson, Fred, was moved to Seattle, Washington, to dwell and live with an aunt, one of Cres's sisters, when he was high school age. This move didn't align with my better judgment but I was out-voted by my own wife, my two sisters-in-law and my brother-in-law. Well, I was only married to the mother, and I had no actual blood relationship with him. They were a family. In passing, let me point out that our home banking system might have taught a lesson to my other sons. Manuel, my eldest, working just a year out of college and still unmarried, bought himself a home. Marcel, about a year after marriage invested in real estate. And my older stepson, Rhu, also lives in his own house. Fred is still unsettled, living a life without a plot.[111]

Previously, I referred to a family plan that required that I, as the head, would assume the responsibilities for managing the household expenses. All bills therefore fell in my lap; I also did all the marketing,[112] and to guarantee that there was an eternal supply of "chicken on the table," my better half totally washed her pinkies of these chores. There was some flaw in this arrangement, however. I became a compulsive buyer. I would go grocery shopping for eggs, and I would come home with whatever else was at discount prices.

Once, Cres decided to display her culinary expertise and while looking for the ingredients to fit her feast she discovered that the fridge was packed with supplies that would last to eternity. She reprimanded me for my extravagance and also determined that on our next trip to Safeway, she would definitely take charge. On our succeeding safari to the store, she took the helm and vowed not to spend more than $10.00, the amount she stashed in her purse. To the store we went, she picking and loading the cart which I volunteered to steer. When we lined up at the check counter, I sneaked back, hiding behind some boxes, knowing that her budget fell far short of the expenditures. The cashier had just half-way punched the groceries when my wife realized that her cash was insufficient, so she looked around for me but could not find me. I was intently observing her from my hiding place. When I watched her embarrassment, I, like a genie, appeared to save the lady in distress. That experience made her vow never to indulge in a marketing expedition. To the present day, she still finds it difficult to separate beef from pork or chicken from rabbit. Cres performed her household chores dutifully, cleaning the house, washing the clothes, and seeing that the children were raised properly. But for many years, she never offered to pay for most household needs and necessities. She dismissed all bills and household, transportation, and other costs, leaving it to me to handle.

One year, I went to visit the homeland, leaving Cres behind with the kids. During one of my days away from home, she decided to visit her sister living just 50 miles away from Salinas. On her return trip, she was hit by another car driven by an elderly man. Not knowing what course to pursue, she panicked. Agitated and anxious, Cres called me long distance to the Philippines with the bad news. I advised her to calm down, and that everything would be settled upon my returning home. She was so alarmed, not knowing what, when, where, and how. I came home expecting to face a complicated situation which required a pocketful of mazuma for settlement. To my relief and peace of mind, the damage to the car was less than the cost of the long-distance phone call to me in the Philippines. She also repeatedly indulged in calling her relations overseas, Canada and across the dear USA during my absence. So the single bill that interested her was the phone bill. If it was exorbitant, she would keep it from me.

It was my usual routine to gather all household bills at the end of the month, so that they were properly accounted for and financially settled. In most cases, the Pacific Telephone statement was lacking. After reminding her that the telephone company has a policy to cut services if they are not paid, and that it takes time to reconnect services, she produced the missing papers and vowed to pay them from her expense account. Of course, without duress, I settled the bill.

Some years after my eightieth year of troublesome life, I realized that the unexpected inevitable could happen at any time. I pressured Cres to learn to cope with the demands of the family finances. We mutually agreed to open a checking account at a bank of her choice in her name only. She had to learn how to balance her account; she had to acquaint herself with the handling of our household expenses. All this was designed to prepare her for the day she would become the titular matron of a household.

As was expected, she found it difficult to balance her accounts. There were times when the bank opened her eyes wide with the expletive warning: "insufficient funds." Her records didn't always tally with the ledgers of the bank, and she could never completely fathom how it happened. In most instances, her records were in the black compared to the red in the bank records. I would have to reconcile and review her checking records, and in many cases, I discovered that she would write and issue checks which were not recorded, or would add expenses in lieu of subtracting them. Thankfully, she was determined to learn and these days, she is able to face the problem squarely. It is a rare month when she now seeks my assistance. Our personal checking accounts are now merged, she, handling most transactions. She is completely ready to handle a household when the inevitable comes knocking at the door.

After I retired from the Department of Corrections in 1972, my wife was still employed in her chosen profession. She begged me to stay at home and enjoy my retirement. She wanted me to abandon and forget my social and community involvement. That was her point of view on retirement. Contrariwise, I didn't fully subscribe to her thinking, or her wishes. I warned her that if I did what she asked, I would quickly be walking to an early grave. Therefore, I continued to perform, although not very actively, in my secondary avocations, real estate broker, insurance salesman, tax preparer, notary public, immigration and naturalization consultant, and even a travel agent. When my licenses in these trades expired in 1988, I decided not to renew them, so that looking back at my remunerative working years, I see no regrets.

My social and community involvement, however, continues to the present day. I visualize no end of these charitable participations—I pray and hope—until the end of my life.
My beloved wife also retired in 1986 after twenty-three years of service at local hospitals. I reminded her of her advice to stay home at retirement, but she could not follow her own advice. Both retired ("retarded" is how we describe our retirement), we are free as the wind, spending more time away from home than in.

Our children, all grown-ups with families of their own,

ceaselessly urge us to enjoy our retirement. Whenever we are together or any of these children are visiting us, we hear them urge us: "Mom, Dad, you worked so hard during your hay days. Now is the time for you to enjoy life. Travel, go places, satisfy your desires, spend whatever you managed to save on yourselves. You need not worry about us; we can manage on our own. We are mature adults, mindful of our responsibilities. We need not depend on you. You raised us to be responsible sons, of which we are grateful, so live the life of Riley."

My wife and I would like in many ways to take seriously their message of travelling and seeing the world, but these days, our health and physical condition will not cooperate. Live luxuriously, we also dreamed. We are just a couple raised in poverty —immune to the fancy life—and discarding our roots scares us. We are simple people with simple wants, period.

We are both retired now. Our nest egg is comfortably sufficient to allow us to live the simple life we enjoyed during our working years. We have not yet bothered our children for help or for financial assistance. They have assumed family responsibilities and they are coping with these obligations with flying colors. They made us contented grandparents to boot.

Manuel Luz Jr., the elder (BS, Aeronautical Engineering and an MBA, management, and now a "fisher of men") sired two sons: Eric and Justin. Marcel, the younger (attended California State University, Sacramento, and has shifted his banking experience to his present career as a peace officer) has a son, Nicholas. Robert, my oldest stepson (an artist and painter) is raising a daughter, Rhani. Fred, the stepson who was snatched from my care by my in-laws, Fred has three children: Michael, Adam, and Christopher.[113]

My niece, Editha, the only close relative allowed to join me in the United States, has been like a daughter to me. She remains my line of communication to our relatives in the Philippines. She is also comfortably married with a daughter, Arlene (Ph.D in psychology and a university professor), and a son, Eric (BS, Industrial Engineering and MBA, management). We love our family dearly and we explicitly believe they love us without doubt. My wife and I are enjoying the sunset of our lives in peace and with the love of our children and grandchildren.

My paramount and deepest regret is that when my ship of state sails into the sunset, I will not be able to bequeath to my loved ones the big treasure at the end of the rainbow, the sunshine that never sets, and all the joys from the fountain of youth. All I can bestow to them are useless riches like the silver in my hair, the rings under my eyes, the gold in my teeth, the gas in my stomach, the stones in my kidneys, the lead in my feet, and the abundant love in my heart.

"Love is a many-splendored dose of sex appeal with a little moonlight for sweetness. Taken properly, it adds glitter in the eyes, sparkle on the cheeks, and more vitamins in the blood. Taken improperly, it causes crying and wailing and the return of engagement rings." unknown

8. LIFE STORIES

My father was full of stories. A lifetime of adventures and experiences will do that to you. From his exploits returning to the Philippines to encounters with people across America, my dad had many insightful tales to tell. But behind the stories were lessons learned and lessons imparted. There were morals to the story—about pride and avarice and intolerance and how to treat your fellow man. It was in the listening beyond his stories that true wisdom could be attained.

Sir, you cannot put me in a place worse than I have been before, nor discriminate against me worse than I have been discriminated before."

That, in a nutshell, was my ready answer when applying for a government job and warned about the undue treatment I might receive from other employees of the institution. Proudly, I broke the race barrier, and was the first Filipino to be employed by the California Department of Corrections.[114]

I have been subjected to a lot of indignities, hatred, and undue insults by other ethnic groups and races. I became steeled and immune to these disgraceful, un-Christian attitudes. I dismissed them with the thought that they knew not what they did: "To understand all is to forgive all." I felt that if they could only understand the Filipinos, they would know better and rethink their antagonistic behavior. Once they learned more of the Filipinos—as happened during World War II—attitudes would made a turn for the better, and we would receive more positive treatment.

But looking backward, the worst treatment I was ever subjected to was not at the hands of the Anglos or any other nationalities, but by my own people, and their inconsiderate and unfriendly holier-than-thou attitudes. Filipinos should know their own *kababayans*.[115] But no, some put up airs of superiority, believing that perhaps worldly possessions, education and intellectual learnings, or political considerations give them the license to look down on me, a mere peon struggling to make a decent living.

During World War II, I was part of a contingent of citizen-soldiers stationed at Michigan University in Ann Arbor. We were there to complete specialty courses that would contribute to the ultimate disarmament of the Japanese Imperial Army. We were billeted in the campus dormitories, studying and performing the duties and training of any regular army men. We were Military Intelligence Personnel[116] being prepared to be the first wave of American soldiers to invade mainland Japan.

There were of course, parties and programs outside of regular Army routine, offered for the entertainment of the troops. Naturally, the citizenry were the sponsors, and the soldier-students were honored guests. At one particular campus activity, a multi-cultural presentation, I was introduced to a number of Filipina students whom I later learned were "Full Bright Scholarship" recipients. I had never met a group of so-called intellectuals who were more arrogant, rude, and inconsiderate. We were just a couple of Filipinos in Army attire, members of the Army Specialized Training Program, but we were totally ignored by these "Filipina scholars," avoiding us at every turn, and yet they surely enjoyed the company of the others, preferably the pale faces. Lucky for us, the other Pinoy and I, there were hordes of coeds who gave their time to entertain us; they showed great respect to us in uniform.

Why did they react to us like we were garbage, a contagious disease, or something worse? Was it because we were just non-commissioned officers? It could not be, for almost all of us citizen-soldiers were privates and NCOs. Was it because they believed that, as soldiers, we were not fit to grace the tables of the intellectuals? Little did they know that the majority of the soldiers in their midst were college graduates (some with PhDs), professionals, and business executives, and that there was no member of our contingent who had not attended a US college or university. In other words, we were, in a sense, also *pensionados*[117] just like these arrogant, inconsiderate Filipino "scholars." Pity them, Oh Lord, they knew not what they were doing.

The treatment I was subjected to in Ann Arbor reminded me of several instances on the west coast that put a damper extraordinaire. Some *pensionados* sent to America to further their studies would not tarry longer than a day or so in San Francisco, Seattle, or Los Angeles even with family friends and relatives because as they proclaimed, "I don't want to be mugged," implying that west coast Filipinos were all ruffians and scoundrels. This attitude was a blunt insult to us Filipinos residing in the Pacific states. The origin of these unkindly proclamations emanates from our own native land, from our own people, who have never known of the really peaceful and tranquil nature of us Filipinos. Hurting to the bones, indeed!

On the other side of the picture, let me also mention that many Pacific states Filipinos housed, entertained, and served many visitors, tourists, and cultural groups, sometimes days or weeks, without cost to these cormorants. And then these tourists or visitors would leave their benefactors with nary a word of gratitude. Yet, when we become *balikbayans*,[118] we practically gave our souls to those for whom we enjoyed their company. We managed to pay our way—our way was to please and pay for our needs and our family and guests.

From the time the Philippine government opened offices in San Francisco in the early 1950s, I have had several occasions to personally visit the Philippine Consulate.[119] As I had many business-related visits at their offices, I consequently acquired the personal acquaintances of some of the people there, including the Consul-General. My position as a Filipino community leader perhaps opened my access to the inner office, by-passing most of the clerks. Whenever a Filipino student, trader or visitor wanted to come to Salinas, the Philippine Consulate, San Francisco, would invariably direct them to contact me at my humble home.

There were Filipino nationals studying in various universities in California whose studies included the development of the agricultural industry, who were referred to me by the Philippine Consulate Office in San Francisco. One particular student from UC Berkeley, had the gall to write me and call me by phone directing me to write for her a dissertation regarding the agricultural situation, past and present, in the Salinas Valley. She wanted it as an inclusion to her thesis, the role of the *pinoys* in the development of the agricultural industry in California. Perhaps I could have consented to act according to her schemes, but to be approached, not in person and not knowing the person, I decided to ignore her request. She was the only person I remember who received no help from me.

I had personally directed these students to the resources they sought, updating them on the roles which we Filipinos played in the development of agriculture, or relating to them the ups and downs of Filipino life. Foremost among these students whose research and studies centered on life in the Salinas Valley was Edwin Armirol, who ultimately became a Professor at California State University, Davis, Department of Asian Pacific Studies. Two or three days, often more, these young people became my charges. Except for Professor Armirol, these students disappeared from my life forever. No word of thanks for all these rendered services.

The Philippine Consulate in San Francisco was very grateful for my generous assistance to their two representatives who were assigned to Monterey County to register Filipinos. In the 1960s, there was an initiative by the Philippine government to register all Filipinos who chose to spend their lives in America. For several days, under the request of the Consulate, I assisted them in the performance of their mission. I took them to the labor camps, to homes, or wherever Filipinos took residence, and I assisted them in filing registration forms, and notarizing them as required (free, of course). I was later informed that the most successful drive was in Monterey County.[120]

However, during that decade, I also experienced very uncomplimentary treatment by several Consular personnel. It happened during a baptismal party at the home of a mid-management officer of the Consulate. An uncle of the child's father and I drove to San Francisco and arrived before the christening party returned from church. People from the Stockton area also came simultaneously with our arrival. Filipinos from the rural areas, i.e., the people from the agricultural fields, were the first guests to attend the celebrations.

When the Consulate staff, mostly the clerical upstarts, began to arrive, they were greeted by the presence of rural residents from Salinas and Stockton. Seeing that we were "country mice" and not "city dudes," they shied away from us, gathering together as an elite clique, casting seemingly leery looks upon us. We began to realize that we were treated like garbage by these government servants.

Eventually, the rest of the Consulate staff began to arrive at the party. One of these latter arrivals was one of the ladies whom I had several days of pleasure escorting and aiding in the registration of Filipinos in my own agricultural community. She didn't hesitate to come and greet me, shaking my hand like I was a long-lost relative. She said, within hearing distance, "How are you, Mr. Luz, and how is business progressing?"

Responding with a very positive but humble reply, I announced, "Thank God, I am feeling great, and the business is doing appreciably good and progressing." She told those around us that I was a bachelor unattached, had a real estate and insurance business, and that I also managed the Philippine Trading Company, a dry goods merchandising concern. A real dumper to their superiority complex. Those from the Consulate office who initially ignored my company then inched their way back to my corner. I became like a lump of *tagapulot*,[121] attracting the swarming ants. I talked and listened amicably to them but inside me, they were just inconsiderate "better than-thou" bigots. While they now treated me with respect, they continued to display a lack of consideration and tolerance for others. And the irony of the situation was that they were part and parcel of the Diplomatic Service—no tact and diplomacy!

Another encounter with the lack of consideration and tolerance from my own countrymen took place in Honolulu, Hawaii, in December 1947. I was a passenger on the SS President Cleveland on its maiden voyage to the Orient and Manila. I was going back to the homeland not only to share my happiness with my family, but also to explore the possibility of moving back there permanently. Honolulu—Aloha Land—was the first port-of-entry, a two-day stop for refueling, taking on cargo, and unloading freight. Meeting me at port was my very good friend, George Almarez, a business entrepreneur, newspaper man, and one of the local-Filipino leaders. He was the one who supplied me with Filipino movies which I screened for Filipinos at the Salinas Globe Theater and the Alisal Movie House. He also arranged and booked Filipino cinema stars to accompany their movies. In Honolulu, he showed me the whole town, including tourist attractions and Filipino businesses, and he also introduced me to some of their leaders. The afternoon prior to our departure to Manila, he brought me and another co-passenger to pay a visit to one of the best-known Filipinos in Honolulu.

The person we were going to visit was the distributor of Philippine films. Arriving at his opulent mansion, we were surprised that he had other guests, also passengers on the President Cleveland. There was a representative from the Consular Office in San Francisco, a Filipino medical practitioner returning home after intensive advanced courses in the USA, and two well-known, well-heeled Filipino elites. As we entered the rich portals of this house, we first encountered these elites, who were supposedly from well-to-do families from the Eastern Visayas. After the formal introductions, the patriarch of the family, asked us, in a degrading tone, if we were a part of the ship's crew. In our humble manner, we replied unhesitantly and without shame, "No, sir, we are paying passengers."

The answer to his question didn't particularly please him

and his family which included three young damsels, spoiled by their titles and social positions in the Philippines. To him and family, we were mere *utusans*,[122] not fit to be seen on the same platform with him or his family. They were travelling first class and we were only third-class passengers. There existed a dividing line between us, a line we could not possibly cross.

Our host and guide, George, noticed the antisocial air of the situation and he readily coped with the predicament. The medical doctor was next introduced to us. George, in a loud, retaliatory tone, announced, "Doc, Mr. Cacpal (one of my companions) is a flourishing farmer in Central California; he is worth over a quarter of a million dollars. And (pointing to me) this is Attorney Manuel Luz, a respected man of his profession, worth above a half-million US dollars."

The mere mention of big sums of mazuma suddenly cleared the clouds, and believe it or not, the young, snobbish damsels eased themselves back with the sweetest smiles they could muster. After that, we spent hours of good, peaceful dialogue, although my friends and I parried some quite unusual questions. Above all other questions was this: Why did we not live in luxury when we were sufficiently loaded with money? Our surprising answer was that we were immune to living as we were. We didn't want to splurge in luxury which was alien to us. Since we rose to our positions by sweat and brawn, we preferred to spend our extra finances to ease the pangs of poverty of our families back home in the *Pearl of the Orient Seas*. That answer surprisingly made sense to them.

Before we parted company, Cacpal and I were propositioned by the ladies to delay our trip to Manila and keep them company to enjoy the leis and hula-hulas of Aloha land. They entrusted their hush-hush situation to us and planned that they would tarry longer in Honolulu and perhaps enroll for further studies at the University of Hawaii. We regretted not accepting their invitational proposition, but we made a solemn promise that after a few months visit with family and friends, we would come back to them in Honolulu and resume where we left off.

What a sad parting and a solemn vow we did not heartily promise—a promise we had no intention of fulfilling!

It now comes back to me that we spent the Christmas and New Year holidays on board the SS President Cleveland. There were several races or ethnic groups among the list of passengers. The captain initiated a plan to have a holiday party on board ship between San Francisco and Honolulu. The Consulate representative was charged to represent the Filipino passengers in the programming for the party, and he quickly enlisted the two young ladies from the well-heeled families to show Filipino culture at the celebration. Third-class passengers were not invited guests mind you; the party was exclusively, fabulously first class. The morning before the party, the Consulate representative appeared at our third-class recreation room with a very sad face, forlorn with fear. He came to me, an acquaintance of many moons, and bared his broken heart, his fears and shame. The young ladies were suddenly hit by the flu and sore throats, and performing was totally out of the question.

The diplomat pleaded with me to find replacements from among the lowly third-class passengers, but singing, dancing, or playing any instrument did not seem to be among their limited accomplishments. At the eleventh hour, I learned of a young, talented lady amongst us. She was from Los Angeles and had been a professional piano, voice, and song-dance performer. Unassuming and humble, she at first refused. But more pleading from me and the diplomat finally succeeded in persuading her to proudly represent the Filipino passengers. And she did. According to the diplomat,[123] she was superb. Her rendition on the piano and her singing *kundimans*[124] was fabulously applauded by those in attendance.[125]

We left Honolulu according to schedule. As we left port, there was a fire in the boiler room, but it was not threatening enough to bring us back to port. So over the billowing sea, we continued our journey to Manila with high hopes but with uncertainties. Remember, I and the others had been away over two decades.

Many friends, families, and public officials had been urging me to go back to the "only Christian country" in the Orient to live till death takes its toll. And I acknowledge the fact that that thought has been lingering around my mind for longer than I admit. Two areas I had previously visited and explored appealed to me as ideal places to settle down. Malaybalay in the Mindanao Province of Bukidnon and Lucban in the Quezon Province were places that appealed to me because of the weather. Baguio City, climate-wise, was alluring but didn't impress me like the other locations. The climates of these settlements are quite similar to my present residence in Monterey County. But the more time I spent weighing the essentials, the less I could justify my moving back to the Philippines.

There are trillions of things—mostly unpleasant—that I would have to comfortably accept if I decided to relocate. And as an emigree out of the homeland—having lived twice as long away as I actually lived there—the negatives overshadowed the positives. My future discomforts would many times overshadow the comfort the Philippines would offer. These negatives are not based on information supplied by anti-Filipino advocates, but are strictly based on personal experiences and the experiences of other OTs (old timers). I am personally acquainted with a number of unmarried Filipinos and Filipino families who ventured back to the *Pearl of the Orient Seas* with the determined intention to live there for the rest of their lives. They turned their entire assets into cash, sold real and personal properties, uprooted their family trees, and said farewell to our Uncle Sam.[126] The majority of these people came back to good USA—a number in less than a year, some in six months duration. Dissatisfaction of the existing conditions in the homeland drove them back to America.

In my several visits to the Philippines, I experienced and tolerated so many occasions where my fellow countrymen gave me a lack of consideration and tolerance. By nature, I regard myself as an unassuming person who does his best to adjust to prevalent conditions. I try to dance with the music, but many times, the music becomes sour and undanceable. There is always a limit to what you can swallow, and when that hour arrives, you choke. Here are some events that totally dampened my desire to return home for good.

I am accustomed to shopping unchaperoned for personal needs, including clothing, groceries, and food. And when I enter a shop or any establishment, I know and am aware of the cost of the goods I am purchasing. There is no dickering of the cost of items in the USA; they are fixed, period. But in the Philippines, the idea of fixed prices is unknown. Prices are variable. The salesperson, on many occasions, will size up the would-be customer and base the asking price on that evaluation. And coming from abroad, unlearned and inexperienced with the system of valuation, this would multiply your cost considerably. For example, a native would dicker for a bunch of bananas, right before you at a cost of say, two pesos. The customer and salesperson agree conclusively, and the deal is closed. You are next in line, pick up the equivalent bunch of bananas and try to pay at the same rate as the customer who preceded you. But you are shocked to learn that the cost for you would not be two pesos, but twice or thrice that amount. That, in the lingo of the west, is highway robbery. My conscience cannot tolerate such discriminatory treatment.

In the land of the free, I can enter any business establishment. Regardless of how I was dressed, I would generally be greeted by any of the personnel with a happy, "What can I do for you, sir?" or "Have you been served?" Contrariwise in my native land, because I am not of the elite, a known politician, or filthy rich, I would receive no courtesy whatsoever, and eyed like one who could not afford their prices. Again, if there is a line of customers, I would be pushed back in the line, because the mayor's wife or a lady in ermine and big diamond rings must be served immediately. Royalty before the meek and lowly indeed!

In my hometown, Laoag City, I also experienced being treated differently from the native population by the tricycle operators. If I personally and alone engaged these transportation vehicles and even if I carried no luggage, I was charged three or four times more than the others who were loaded with baskets of fish or vegetables. If I refused to pay their *tarifa,*[127] my only alternative was to walk. Indeed, the cost of living as a *balikbayan*[128] grew exorbitantly when "home sweet home."

There have been a number of *kababayans*[129] whose friendships I admired and heartily accepted. A number were tourists or visitors in this country. My wife and I often went out of our daily routine to entertain them at our humble home. We gave them the best we could afford, to make their visits enjoyable and pleasant. We even relinquished our master bedroom for their comfort, and supplied them with whatever was absolutely necessary far beyond and above our own lifestyles. And when they departed to other places, we even gave them extra travel expenses. One family in particular, both professionals, have been our guests every time they crossed the Pacific. And vice-versa, they offered us a room at their Manila residence. Always, they made it a point to visit us, and always they left with extra merchandise and heavier suitcases. However, my wife and I detected that their friendship was rather shallow and even intolerable. When we became their "guests" at their mansion, we were offered a room with a bunkbed, nothing else. We stayed with them only awaiting our schedules to go to the Ilocos or to the Quezon Province. And when we bid farewell to them, we gave appropriate pasalubong (money).

However, my wife and I both felt that our stay with them at their house was not heartily acknowledged, nor was it based on trust, equality and tolerance. We assumed we were good friends—yet we felt that in our relationship, we were not fit to socialize with their local friends. Every time we visited, we were informed in advance that a party at their mansion was planned for the weekend. The advanced notice was an implied suggestion that we would have to vacate the premises days before the shindig. There was never an iota of a desire on their part to have us grace their parties. We actually inquired once from their hired help about their parties, who the guests were and so forth. We learned that there were no big political upstarts, no millionaires, no big executives—just their circle of friends in their professions and some friends who were members of their church. My wife and I got really peeved about this inconsiderate treatment, especially when we recalled some of the parties we had attended in America. In the years I served on many boards and committees, we've rubbed elbows and feasted with business executives, professionals, politicians and statesmen, newspaper publishers and millionaires at their dinners, seminars, and banquets. And yet, we were not fit to be invited to a home party of "friends" in the Philippines.

It is evident that if I ever decide to forsake America and take up permanent residency in the Philippines, I would have to resign myself to a life averse to what I am accustomed to in this land of equality. Let me therefore adhere to my life in the USA—I can live with discrimination by other races, but I cannot live with the biased treatment inflicted on my honor by my own people.

In the early 1950s, the Philippine Republic Department of Labor intended to publish in book form a comprehensive account of labor conditions in the homeland. It was also intended to include the Filipino labor situation in the United States. A certain young *pinay*, a Miss Cruz, was assigned the task of tackling the assignment. Getting direction from the Philippine Consulate General in San Francisco, she was directed to me where I could help her collect date from Salinas and Monterey County. She was assured that I would be able and willing to lend assistance in the completion of her mission.

She arrived in Salinas and booked accommodations at the Cominos Hotel, the biggest and best Salinas had to offer at that period. When Miss Cruz saw that the bellhop was a Filipino, she made immediate inquiry if he knew Manuel Luz. Without hesitation, and not asking why, the bellhop told her that he knew me and that at that particular moment I was engaged in the preparation of food in the kitchen. It was the rush hour for dinner, but the lady insisted that the bellhop tell me that she wanted to talk to me pronto. I sent back word that it was impossible for me to leave my range, but if she could wait, I would be free by nine o'clock that evening. She insisted on seeing me, so we had a peek at each other at the door lobby. Wearing a chef uniform —complete with greasy white jacket and the regular chef hat—I surely surprised her. She was clearly stunned and surprised at my appearance. I reassured her, asking her patience to wait for me until I finished my shift, which was then a little over an hour. I finished my chores at nine, discarded my kitchen garb and dressed myself with my usual garb. I met her at the hotel lobby where she was leisurely perusing magazines.

When I approached Miss Cruz, she could not believe I was the same person she spoke to a little while ago. She was indeed jolted. Nattily dressed in tie and coat,[130] which was the usual daily appearance of Filipinos at that period, I may have appeared to her a very different person, for it took me a period of time to convince her that the cook and the well-dressed Consulate appointee before her were one and the same personalities. I invited her out for chop suey, and as she explaining to me her mission, she admitted to me her disbelief that a Filipino leader trusted by and recommended by the Consular Office could do menial work like sweating behind a sweltering range. This was a strata which was simply alien to Filipino customs in the homeland. I assured her that in America, there is dignity in labor, and that stealing, robbing, or malfeasance were the only undignified professions.

I assured her that if she could put her doubts to rest and show me her complete faith and trust, the undignified culinary laborer could and would assist her to her satisfaction. She admitted that if the Philippine Consulate General could place their confidence on me, she had no alternative but to comply with their recommendation.

For several days, I escorted Miss Cruz to where and what suited her mission. I took her to witness first-hand the laborious task of her countrymen. She interviewed farm workers, visited labor camps, met with labor bosses and Filipino labor contractors. As I drove her around the valley, she noticed that things were different from the homeland. It was not only the vast expanse of agricultural lands, or the way the "rain for rent" irrigation systems operated, or the profuse use of mechanical devices to raise the crops. It was the comradery of the people as well.

One particular day, while driving south on Highway 101 on our way to Gonzales, she noticed a young woman plowing the fields in a John Deere tractor. Her eyes popped out in strange surprise, wondering to herself why a young woman was doing man's work, and in the farms to boot! I assured her that it was common here for a woman to do a man's job; it was not a "novelty." On our way back to Salinas, the lady in the tractor was still lingering in Miss Cruz's thoughts. I told my lady passenger that the tractor driver was perhaps a college student working on a farm owned by her professional father. She tried to dismiss my layman's assessment. Upon reaching the farm where her surprise started, I made a sudden stop and we approached the young lady, who was in the process of turning around the farm. She was kind enough to tarry a little to answer a few questions Miss Cruz wanted to ask. The young lady then told us that she was indeed a college student at UC Berkeley, and that she was the only daughter of the owner/proprietor of the farm. She further offered that her father was a municipal judge in Monterey County and her mother was a leading social worker. We thanked her for her time and for sharing with us the pertinent facts.

The Philippine Department of Labor representative received the hurricane-like surprise of her life. She was deathly jolted and shocked by the information she received from the "farm workers." She could not believe what she was witnessing, seeing, and hearing. I assured her again that in America, working with your hands and earning a living with brawn and sweat were admirable traits—and that there is unquestionably dignity of labor in the land of plenty.

When we arrived in Salinas that day, it was noon, a time for lunch for most workers. While we were cruising downtown, I noticed a group of young men, part of a crew doing road construction work. I suggested to Miss Cruz to talk to a number of these young construction workers. She, at first, hesitated to take my advice, but ultimately, she relented and talked to them. She learned, to her unending surprise, that one of the young men was not only a student, but he had just graduated from college with a degree as a podiatrist. He told my lady companion that he was a self-supporting student, and that he didn't presently possess the finances to open up his practice. His family was financially incapable to help him start his practice, so his only recourse was to earn enough capital to establish his own place of business. Miss Cruz learned something that was utterly contrary to all the practical life in her homeland.

Eventually, we wound up our research and she prepared for her move to other targeted areas. She left Salinas with a different panorama of life—she left with the thought of what makes this country great.

When she had gathered enough materials to satisfy her mission, as well as collected contributions from willing donors, patrons, and advertisers for her project, she bade goodbye to Salinas without looking back. I never heard from her after her departure; even those who gave money for the publication were totally forgotten. Nobody in our locality ever saw a copy of the supposed Department of Labor report. Antecedent to her departure, I admonished her that if she wanted to help her country, she must educate the people on the dignity of labor. I also imparted to her my profound belief that the Philippine people must learn to utilize their upper extremities to keep up with their intellects. I believe strongly that in the Philippines, there prevails thousands of good and beneficial ideas, opinions and thoughts. But their hands—the actions and performance of those ideas—were trailing countless eons behind. The two, brain and hands, must be working closely and side by side together to achieve beneficial results and progress.

◆ ◆ ◆

I have been discussing the dignity of labor demonstrated in this progressive and powerful country, the USA. Such a phenomena is alien to the Republic of the Philippines. On my return visits, I was ridiculed, laughed at, and publicly shamed for doing manual labor.

On my first return home, I discovered that the house where I grew up was in a very shaky and dangerous condition. The posts which hold the house erect and sturdy, were decayed to the point that running your hand through them at ground level would not encounter any obstruction. To ensure the safety of my mother, two sisters, and brother against disasters, like a typhoon or an earthquake, I had no other alternative but to raze the old house and erect another.

I hired some people to help me dismantle the old structure and dismantling, they did. However, the wrecking crew failed to clear the space to erect the proposed sturdy residential structure. Since no one would give me a helping hand—my brother was busy working as a weather observer at the local airport, and an unemployed brother-in-law, a lazy and idle parasite, would not lift a finger—I had to prepare the plot myself. And so, alone, I sorted materials from the old house which could be used for the planned new building. For several days, I labored at this task, and every day, people, many of them students, would stop and linger to watch me do manual labor under the sweltering sun. Whether on purpose or not, I heard many of their comments, "Look at that man working under the hot sun. It is very shameful indeed, especially because he came from the United States. Has he got no shame at all?" I just smiled on the inside and ignored all the uncomplimentary remarks spoken for me to hear. Instead of being complimented for doing an honest day's work for constructive purposes, I was being made the object of their misplaced amusements.

Commencement exercises, the Pomp and Circumstances, was scheduled at my alma mater, the Ilocos Norte High School, from whence the ridiculing students were being educated. The day of graduation, the city mayor—an old friend, co-graduate, cousin, dentist and also a city councilman—picked me up to join the celebrants. The mayor and councilman had reserved seats, but I understood explicitly my position, so I only wanted to linger amongst the masses. The good Mayor had other plans, however. He insisted that a place beside him be prepared for me. So, when I went to occupy the reserved seat, I was the target of all eyes, the center of attention. Soon curiosity became an issue, and hush-hush murmurs came from the multitude. Who I was, who did I represent, and what planet did I come from? Some old acquaintances who knew me quenched their inquisitiveness by openly declaring that I was a trusted amigo of their feared mayor, an alumnus of the Ilocos Norte High School. Others stated that I was an "attorney" from the United States, visiting the old country.[131] That stopped them from being surprised, but the manifestation of my doing menial work only intensified their malicious position that I would not refrain from performing disgraceful occupations. People still stopped and tarried, eyeing me as I finished my project of constructing safe and sturdy housing for my mother and family.

At another time, I spent the weekends at the cottage where my brother, the weather observer, sojourned. With me was my cousin, the city council member. Going back to town, we hitched a ride with a neighbor, a practicing physician. The good doctor's residence was a block away from our own home. Alighting from the truck, I carried a 50 lb. sack of rice and proceeded towards home. I was young and sturdy then and the load was light compared to what I had been doing in the land of opportunity. It was hard for me to believe that my cousin stopped me short, insisting that I drop the sack and put it in a *kalesa*[132] for delivery to the house. Though I assured him that it is no problem, he insisted that my way was a no-no, a shameful act which he could not live with.

There were many other numerous occasions where I witnessed actions which were considered taboo and disgraceful in my homeland, that were considered honest and admirable in my adopted country, the USA.

◆ ◆ ◆

One of the traits of my people is the deeply rooted admiration and respect for titles, more so than for ideals. On one of my visits to the Philippines, I attended a wedding of a fellow Filipino American in my hometown. During the reception, the guests gathered and segregated—the men in one room, the charming ladies in another. In our group were some former acquaintances who were US educated. They were colleagues from Washington, Oregon, and Alaska, who had not forgotten our relationships.

As we enjoyed our reunion, a young man arrived and was immediately introduced to me. As I acknowledged him with the usual greeting, "It is my pleasure to meet your charming acquaintance, sir," I was curtly reminded to call him, "attorney." It was a terrible blow to my ego. However, I gathered my cool and responded, "Pardon me, gentlemen, but if you would kindly lend me your ears, I am more than willing to atone my misgiving. Had you forewarned me of his title or noble profession, I would have heartily respected his professional status."

However," I continued, "let me remind you, as many if not all of you acknowledge, that the Philippine government and education system are strictly patterned after the government and education system of the United States. It is incumbent upon me to tell you, as those of you who have been educated in American universities and colleges know, that the titles, 'Mister' for gentlemen and 'Missus' for gentlewoman, is a sufficient title of respect in American society. I have shaken hands and talked with many distinguished persons, like the governor of California, judges of note, nay, even a member of the nation's high court, and even generals of many professions, and the respectful title of "Mister" is an honorably accepted salutation."

My tirade was abruptly stopped when someone suggested that we change the subject.

Later, during that same sojourn in Laoag City, I had nothing to do but idle my time, so I attended some court sessions by the Provincial Courts of First Instance (similar to US Superior Court). One day, the high court was convened to plan the court calendar. I was amused by the actions of one of the attorneys who was present at the wedding party. I had been informed that this young legal mind was top of his class when he passed the Philippine bar exams. Addressing the court and his colleagues, he was gaveled by the presiding judge when he referred to the other attorneys as "Mister."

He was actually saying the very points I mentioned at the party in front of this court of law. In short, he was pronouncing that the Philippines should follow the US and other democratic nations in putting people on equal terms by simply using the title of "Mister." The judge finally ruled that the word "attorney" before a name could be omitted, but instead, the word "esquire" would be required after the name.

Another experience I encountered during a vacation in the Philippines dealt with health. An old friend, a tailor, lived in the house across the street from the house I built for my mother, brother, and sisters. Every day he complained of a migraine headache; as a result, he spent most of his time in bed, forcing himself to follow his means of livelihood. I had met the two doctors simultaneously treating him. The only remedy that was prescribed by these two medical practitioners was some pills, maybe aspirin—but the headache persisted to bother him. One day, when he was feeling chirpy and hearty, I invited him for a walk to the center of town. We strolled around the business area, window shopped, and greeted friends. I saw the sign I was searching for—an optometrist. I took my friend by the hand and urged him to follow me. The office was on the second floor of the building, and he was wondering what my mission was. But before I could explain, we were face-to-face with the doctor's charming office assistant. The eye specialist met with us and I pointed to him that my companion needed to have his eyes examined. Reluctantly, my friend submitted to the tests. But as the examination progressed and different lenses were tested, my friend excitedly shouted, "Pare! I see very clearly and distinctly!"

"That is why I brought you here, my friend," I responded, "To help you see clearer."

Eyeglasses were prescribed for him; however, the glasses had to be ordered from Manila, so they arrived a week later. I coached my friend to "wear them and never take them off except when going to sleep or taking a bath. Never mind the itch on the ear or on the bridge of your nose. As you get accustomed to them, everything will be grand." As the days came and went, the medical doctors were wondering why my friend never contacted them again. He was proud to tell his doctors the story of his rehabilitation, how I diagnosed his headaches, and best of all, how his tailoring improved in quality and quantity.

Another memorable experience happened on one of my trips from Laoag to Manila. During these days, travelling was a daring experience. Highway hijackers, robbers, and hoodlums were perils on the road. Night travel was out; daylight driving was the only option. Even then, trucks and busses dreaded the travel, so the passengers would pray for no delays on the way. One day, however, the bus on which I was a passenger was registering excessive heat from its radiator. The driver was repeatedly shouting at his assistant, asking him if he had checked the radiator at their last stop, and if water was poured into it. The reply was positive. I heard, as did all the passengers, of the concern of the driver. Finally, I blurted out loudly, "Why don't you stop, open your hood, and check on your engine? Perhaps the fan belt may be loose or broken." They took my advice reluctantly, and coincidentally, they found the fan belt loose and in shreds. The belt was immediately replaced, and the trip proceeded to Manila without further interruption.

The operators of the bus and the passengers were amazed when my analysis of the problem was proven to be fact. I knew what went wrong without even looking over the erring engine.[133] They knew that I was a *balikbayan*.

There were a couple of stores in town, run and operated by former US residents. The National Stores, a cooperative effort of US mainland Filipinos mostly from Salinas, was one of three shops they franchised in the Philippines—one in Manila, one in Pangasinan and one in Laoag City. The other store, Emporium, was owned and operated by other Fil-Americans, mostly Laoaguenians.[134] I used to drop in at the Emporium to luxuriate on their tasty ice creams and halo-halo, good treats especially during sweltering heat. The manager knew that I managed and was part owner of a merchandising establishment in Salinas. So one day, he told me that he was throwing away a lot of ball point pens newly purchased because they would not write. He was blaming the distributors for selling him defective pens. He had boxes full of these pens, and he proceeded to demonstrate to me the uselessness of the stuff.

He had me laughing on the inside as he persistently failed to come up with a workable pen. Finally, I asked him for a match. He knew that I did not smoke; however, puzzled at my request, he produced the item requested. I ignited the match and placed it under the tip of one of his pens, melting and removing the paraffin covering the tip of the pen. Then I told him to write, and the pen magnificently responded. The manager was so grateful for the simplicity of my demonstration, but remorseful of his ineptitude and losses. Happy at the seeming miracle, he then retrieved the pens from the garbage.

.....

"Your greatness is measured by your kindness—your real caliber is measured by the consideration and tolerance you have for others." William J.H. Boetcker[135]

9. MY COMMUNITY SERVICE INVOLVEMENT

My father, having started a family quite late in life, retired at the age of 65, when I was still in junior high school. I remember that he had time to pick me up from school, then make us dinner, before leaving for an evening meeting of one kind or another. It wasn't unusual for him to have evening meetings three or four nights a week. And while I knew these meetings were important, I didn't really understand the scope and depth of what he was doing until I first read this chapter.

In retrospect, I believe that the most fruitful years of my father's life were after he retired. He was able to do what he loved most, which was to serve his fellow man. But then again, this desire fueled him for most of his adult life, all the way back to the 1930s. From helping hundreds of Filipinos obtain their citizenship or help their loved ones immigrate to the US, to the scores of non-profit organizations he served in, his community service involvement was what he lived for.

I initially slipped without fanfare into the Salinas Valley and the City of Salinas during the winter months of 1935. There were just a few people around who I knew or who knew me. Chinatown[136] consequently became my arena of operation. Chinatown was the only place where we Filipinos could browse around freely and safely. Wander onto Main Street or other neighborhoods within the city and you walked into forbidden and dangerous territories. To venture into town to go shopping, or to satisfy yearnings to view a movie,[137] or to satisfy a yen for American cuisine,[138] was to take your life in your hands. Some establishments managed by Chinese entrepreneurs would offer service to us Filipinos. But generally, we had to go in numbers for safety reasons and for protection. Chinatown was the sin district to many, and to many Filipinos, Soledad Street was Chinatown. It was a "boulevard of broken dreams."

America, the land of the free and the home of the brave, encourages the populace to acquire better and higher education.

It is the key to a successful and fruitful life in the United States. But at that time, this principle was only applicable to Anglo, white-skinned citizens. It was not meant to include us Filipinos. There were more than dozens of Filipinos who managed by hard work and sacrifice to complete required college courses. Many were from US colleges and universities, but they were given the opportunity to practice their acquired skills. Hence, they stooped back to Chinatown. They were among those who lived on Soledad Street, Salinas, California, the "boulevard of broken dreams."

Labor Organization Activities

Winter in the Salinas Valley translated to no activity on the farms. The wintery weather, with the rains and the cold, was not conducive to farm activities. In the 1930s, Filipinos dominated the stoop labor in the agricultural fields, and those Filipinos who opted not to follow the crops to the Imperial Valley or Arizona, remained domiciled in the labor camps run by domineering Filipino straw bosses, who spent most of their leisure time in Chinatown. I came to Salinas with double intentions. One was to work in the fields and to build lasting friendships with my fellow countrymen. But I came also with an ulterior motive, to organize the field workers into a union with the end in-view of bettering wages and living conditions. Before coming to Salinas, I had experienced working with some labor leaders and I had gained some insight within the labor union activities. The UCAPWA,[139] a movement that embraced field workers from the Pacific Coast to Louisiana, was the focal point of our activities. I was affiliated with the AFL[140] and later with the CIO,[141] and the latter helped finance my labor activities.

Living on Soledad Street was not as cheap as one might think. I became a sort of a partner with other *pinoys* who managed a small business. We sold made-to-measure suits representing a tailoring business out of Los Angeles. But the business was so slow due to the lack of work, and money was scarce.

Those days, however, the Filipino farm worker never dared be seen in the streets not dressed in made-to-measure suits and colorful matching ties. The custom was that jackets were worn only to go to work, and ready-made suits were cheaper and abundant in the stores. But no, the Filipino would rather be dead than be seen without his made-to-measure suit. When the season started and paychecks would come in regularly, the suit business boomed upward.

I became very friendly with one of my customers. He urged me to stay with him in a small labor camp within walking distance from town. From there, I could come to town, when not working, and struggle to establish the organization of the agricultural workers, along and with the Anglo organizers who represented the shed workers. We had an office on Market Street, next door to the then Togo Dry Cleaners.

However, my labor union activities infuriated the Filipino farm labor bosses (who to me, were stooges of the farmers, growers, and shippers), and also made me a marked man by the townspeople, especially the growers. I was barred from the labor camps and black-listed by them. I could not return to my status as a farm labor contractor in Kern County, where I was once ordered to pack up all my gear within 24 hours and leave town. People there blamed us Filipinos for lowering wages and wrestling away jobs from them.[142] We were just trying to eke out a living.[143] In a nutshell, I was a persona non grata in Salinas. But such a welcome did not deter me from making the decision to become a permanent resident of this green-gold country. I slowly but persistently worked myself into the good graces of the Filipinos and the citizenry. I respected the laws, obeyed them, and did my sincerest best to help the Filipino. But to live in this valley, I had to disavow any connections with the labor movement.

Immigration Service and Activities

So much of the social changes toward Filipinos in the

valley are because of World War II. Labor bosses—who showed no affection to me, and some of them totally ignoring my existence—turned around and manifestly accepted me after the war. This very radical metamorphosis of their personal attitudes actually shocked me. Some of them actually encouraged their men (Mexican nationals) to shop at the Philippine Trading Company, a merchandising concern which I helped establish and manage.

It was also because of World War II that Filipinos were allowed to file for citizenship.[144] It was a requirement that all applicants for US citizenship attend citizenship classes and be sponsored or witnessed by two American citizens. But Filipinos who were naturalized US citizens were hard to find or locate in those days. Most of the ones who became US citizens were still serving in the Armed Forces. Since I was readily visible, accessible and omnipresent in Salinas, I became a witness for hundreds of my countrymen, helping them obtain their US citizenship. Among them were the very labor bosses who branded me a traitor to my homeland.[145] My position as a witness for many Filipinos in their citizenship proceedings greatly enhanced my acceptance in the Filipino Community of Salinas Valley. Sometimes, I sat all day long in the jury box, a place for witnesses. After a while, Judge Jorgensen, the presiding judge, even memorized my citizenship number which I, myself, didn't know by heart.[146]

Service to the American Legion

Probably my most important and most rewarding community involvement decision—though taken reluctantly—was my opting to join the American Legion. Specifically, it was to organize a Filipino Post, Fil-Am Post 652, in equal footing with any other post in the American Legion. The greatest motivating factor that influenced me in joining this great patriotic organization was their motto: "The American Legion cherishes four great principles: justice, freedom, democracy and loyalty." As such, we were pledged to serve the disabled, the distressed, the widowed and the orphaned. We were devoted to the cause of service to the community, the state, and the nation. All of these were corollaries to everything I dreamed of and hoped to live for.

When we, the Filipino War Veterans—with the unrelenting efforts of the American Legion district officers of District 13, Department of California (Monterey, Santa Cruz, San Benito, Santa Clara, and San Mateo counties)—received our Charter as Fil-Am Post 652, the corps of officers was also installed as prescribed by the Post's Constitution and By Laws. The meeting was well attended by Legionnaires from the 13th District, representing more than thirty posts. The Filipino veterans were extremely grateful by the show of unexpected acceptance of their Filipino comrades-in-arms.

As the newly installed Commander of Fil-Am Post 652, I was expected to deliver my acceptance speech, both for the charter of Post 652 and for my newly exalted position. Nervous and shaky was I, for although I had spoken publicly many times, it was mostly in the presence of my countrymen. This crowd was not the piney group; it consisted mostly of Anglos and most of them were professionals, business people, learned and financially settled. I had to say a silent prayer prior to gathering enough gumption to stand tall and talk. My fears, however, totally faded when I saw their faces, nodding acceptance to what I was saying. In other words, their acceptance of my address was a huge boast to my ego. After the meeting, everyone shook my hand, telling me how pleased they were to hear me. It was as if I had opened their hearts and minds as to what we Filipinos could do and accomplish.

Soon, the things that had happened and what was said, and how we Filipino Veterans conducted ourselves, spread throughout the whole District. Local Legionnaires, officers, and members would introduce me as the Commander of the newly chartered Fil-Am Post 652. In all those Legion activities, I often listened to praises regarding my "inaugural speech." I became sort of a celebrity in the 13th District, Department of California, The American Legion. Until recently when age got the best of me, I had attended district meetings, area meetings, Department of California conventions and national conventions. And I had the rare distinction of being a perennial delegate of Fil-Am Post 652 to district meetings, area meetings and Department of California State conventions.[147]

We were initially part and parcel of the 13th District, Department of California. The District grew by leaps and bounds and membership grew, which made it impossible for the District Commander to visit all the Posts. We asked the Department in Convention assembled to split the District; our request was unanimously granted, hence, the 28th District was born. Attending all 13th District and later 28th District meetings and activities had placed me in a position where almost all active Legionnaires, within these geographical boundaries, accepted me as one of them and in equal footing with everyone. I was honored to have served as the second Legionnaire elevated as Commander of the tremendous 28th. A few years later, I was requested, nay, pushed, to accept a spot in the 28th District Executive Board. I had to discard my "blue cap," a uniform which is the symbol of membership in the American Legion, in place of the blue cap with a white top, symbolic of the new position, and it became my prize possession. From this responsibility, I advanced through the successive chairs until I was elevated to the Commandership of the 28th District, which was also a position in the Department Executive Council. These positions also required me to attend American Legion meetings in other sections of the State.

Aside from this top District assignment, I have served my jurisdiction in such standing committees as: Membership; Judge Advocate, serving under different Commanders; Naturalization; Un-American activities; Americanisms; Child Welfare Resolutions and Constitution and By-Laws; and Community Services. I also served in the District Trial Board for three years, a position which is appointed by the California Department Commander under concurrence of the Executive Board.

In the year 1953, the 28th District Department of California, I was in a position to place a member for nomination and election for the coveted position as Vice-Commander (Area Commander) for the entire Department. I was again strongly urged by many Legionnaires to throw my hat in the ring. I succumbed to their insistence. A primary election within the District was conducted to pick the District's choice and the winner's name was to be placed in nomination at the Department Convention in Sacramento. There were three very active, highly motivated, good Legionnaires opposing me. One was an educator, the second the manager of a big department store, and the third a distributing agent for a chain of bakeries. When the votes were finally tallied, the name, Manuel L. Luz, was declared the unanimous winner.

There were some oppositions, especially from San Francisco, against my candidacy. The foremost and most prevalent reason for the opposition was none other than my ethnic background and most importantly, my accent. They searched extensively for someone who would run against my "Filipino accent," but at the Sacramento convention, the opposing Districts failed to nominate an anti-Luz candidate. From what eventually happened, I knew that my unblemished accomplishments as a Legionnaire prevailed in appeasing the opposition.

My name was presented to the convention and a white ballot was cast in my favor. This placed me as the first Filipino in the continental USA to be elevated to such a distinguished position. The one-year term was a grueling one, requiring dedication, time, and money. I relinquished the position at the 1954 Convention in Hollywood. Several Legionnaires I met throughout the state urged me and promised their solid support if I would opt for the highest Department position. My experiences during the whole year plus the expenses (which I could not afford) were sufficient reasons for a negative answer. One year as a "white cap" Legionnaire was enough.

As a perennial delegate to the Department of California conventions, I marched with my comrades in most parades of Legionnaires, an important feature of the conventions. These extravaganzas featured decorated floats, motorcycles in systematic and intricate formation, drum and bugle corps, marching bands, baton twirlers, and legionnaires both healthy and disabled in wheelchairs—all marching in groups under the colors of their own Districts. With hundreds in mass formation, the individual becomes unrecognized and unnoted. My own individual pride in these parades, where I stood clearly in the limelight, was during my last week as a "white cap" Legionnaire.[148] Hollywood Boulevard was the parade route, for the convention was held at the American Legion Stadium. The parade was led by massed flags, both the stars and stripes and the American Legion flags. The Department Commander open car followed by the then six Vice Commanders sitting atop convertible Cadillacs. When our contingent passed the review stand, the Vice Commanders were rushed to their positions to lead their massed Legionnaires from their own areas.

I marched proudly, leading my Second Area Legionnaires through that famed boulevard. And I could see the faces—some surprised and astonished—to watch this large contingent of Legionnaires being led by a "little brown monkey."

After reverting to a "blue hat" Legionnaire, I never had any desire to again run for any high position. I only wanted to serve my fellow Legionnaires at the Post level. Nevertheless, I have been honored by appointments to serve my 28th district and the Department of California in various permanent commissions and committees, as I had already mentioned. My appointments and selections to serve also expanded to the national organization, including nominations to the Membership Advisory Committee, Foreign Relations Committee, and Counter-Subversive activities of the National American Legion.

Service to Hospital and Health Care Organizations

In the years prior to 1980, tuberculosis was a prevalent, dreadful, and contagious disease. It was a sickness which made unacceptable applicants for immigration to America. All applicants for visas were x-rayed and any applicant showing signs of TB would be automatically denied. Monterey County Hospital-Natividad Hospital maintained an isolated ward for TB patients. There were also several patients of Filipino extraction in the local hospital wards. The Monterey County Tuberculosis and Health Association was organized to help the struggle to conquer this contagious disease. The programs of this Association were to educate the citizenry about TB, and to raise funds for research for total control and elimination of this microbe from the face of the globe. TB organizations were active in all parts of the state, if not world-wide. As a part of their charter, the Association invited guest speakers from different countries with grave problems involving TB to their regular sessions.

Once a speaker from the Philippines was sought. Several Filipino health practitioners, doctors, and nurses were approached, but to their dismay, not one accepted the invitation. So, they directed their attention to the local Filipino leaders. Many were asked, but still nary a soul dared the challenge. In desperation and through recommendations by many Filipinos, they contacted me. I knew I was not knowledgeable in any health program, most importantly TB, but I had had personal contacts with people in the Philippines suffering the ravages of the disease. I had occasions also to have visited Filipino patients in Salinas TB wards. I still am in a cloud as to why I accepted their invitation to speak.

With shaky and unsteady legs, and with very vague knowledge and understanding of the subject, I mumbled and jumbled, hoping to hit the "nail on the head" and satisfy their minimum expectations of me. I ended my scatter-brained dissertation, thinking what an *ass* I was to have appeared here. I was sweating in shame and wanted to disappear hastily into oblivion. But to my unexpected relief, I was heartily received, to the point that almost every soul who quietly heard my presentation came and shook my sweaty hands. I was further amassed by the turn of events at that meeting. All the members of the TB Executive Board unanimously voted me to serve with them as a member of the Governing Board.

Thus, I became part and parcel of their activities. Being the only Filipino in the movement—I say only Filipino because I have never encountered another countryman in all the forums and conferences in all parts of the State—I was delegated to translate into Filipino some of the pamphlets on TB, a task I hesitatingly accepted due to limited comprehension of our many vernaculars. I had, however, privately engaged the assistance of other Filipino linguists. I ended my time with the TB Association after three consecutive terms—to fulfill obligations with other social services.

After my stint with the Monterey Tuberculosis and Health Association, I never thought I would be again involved personally in the health care of my fellow citizens. But the unforeseen future had other schemes for me. Some years later, I answered a phone call from the Salinas Valley Memorial Hospital.[149] The caller identified himself as a member of the hospital, Ben Lopez, a community leader who served side by side with me on the Community Action Advisory Committee, Employment Development Department for the State of California. He was inviting me to join Him in the proposed SVMH Administrative Committee. I was still vague as to the real responsibilities and objectives of this proposal, but curiosity propelled me to attend. There was a dozen of us from all parts of the Valley. At the meeting, it was expounded that "funds" would be the core of our work, to raise and direct expenditures. With unanimous endorsement, we proceeded to elect officers so work could, without delay, proceed. With intense reluctance, I was chosen as Secretary of the Committee, an office I filled for two years.

The workload of this committee and the need for new ideas prompted the committee and the hospital administration to increase the membership of our Administrative Committee. The Board of Governors was designed and incorporated under the corporate laws of the State of California. Its personnel were also increased to 43 citizens from all walks of life, but mostly professionals, business executives and agriculturists. Several of the new Governors were very well-to-do and/or millionaires. The contacts with the citizenry—rich, poor, or in-between—widened and expanded by leaps and bounds. Millions of shining dollars poured into hospital funds through direct contributions by wills and testaments. Even real estate was donated to the health facility.

The sum total of the funding from these yearly campaigns led to the construction of added new units to the hospital, and refurnishing the original structure, the foremost being the Heart Center.[150] A 300-car garage was also constructed for the convenience of visitors and families of hospital patients. The newest of medical equipment, medical techniques, and innovative procedures were acquired which by the 1980s put our Salinas Valley Memorial Hospital on par with the most modern hospitals in America.

Not long after my service with the Board of Governors in SVMH, I was approached to serve in the same capacity by the then Salinas Community Hospital, which was owned and operated by a group of local medical doctors. Again, the "sucker that I am" accepted the challenge. However, at that particular time, the Hospital was struggling due to growing financial setbacks. The Board of Governors could not compete with the Board of Governors at SVMH. The Salinas Community Hospital consequently breathed its last—and locked its doors forever. Efforts to revive this needed facility in East Salinas failed, and its demise was lamentably missed by its clientele, especially those who could not afford the comforts of SVMH.

Service To Social Organizations

The Anti-Poverty Coordinating Council of Monterey County served the poor during the late 1960s-1970s. This group was financed by the federal government and from grants by other philanthropic agencies or corporations. Their operations were housed at the Glicbark Building, corner of Main and Gabilan Streets, in Salinas. They occupied the entire second floor of the structure. As the name implied, their operations were specially geared to serving the poor, to find employment for the unemployed, put roofs over the heads of the homeless, and to encourage the establishment of small businesses for the populace. The members of the coordinating council were, except for the executive director, from all walks of life, representatives from the various ethnic groups and serving gratis.

The operation of the Council was already in progress when I was tapped to join and add my two-cents worth in this "labor of love." My dream of helping the down-trodden forced me to accept their invitation. As a legitimate member, I gave it my utmost best to contribute and in no time, I was elevated to the Executive Board of the service organization. The operations continued until funds were no longer available.

We faced a lot of problems mostly on the division and allocation of funds. One group indeed, the Hispanic sector, demanded more than their share; they demanded to control programs and of course, they clamored for a Latino director. The organizational director was Anglo, replaced by an Afro-American whose term was replete with financial anomalies, then supplanted by a Latino to appease the clamor of the members.[151] It was during the incumbency of the Latino executive that things became worse and uncontrollable. Due to the unavailability of funds, the Anti-Poverty Coordinating Council was ordered to close shop. There were five of us, including government-appointed personnel, that worked to phase out the programs of the Council and to make a full accounting of the books.

Again, an important and necessary program was relegated to extinction because of excessive demands—nay, greed—of the beneficiaries themselves.[152]

Out of the ashes of the Anti-Poverty Council emerged the Community Services Commission of Monterey County, an extension of the United States Services Administration. This Community Services Commission was composed of citizens appointed by the members of the Monterey County Board of Supervisors. The then County Supervisor, ex-mayor of Salinas, Attor-

ney Atteridge, named me to the Commission. Two succeeding supervisors, Reverend Morris and Barbara Shipnuck had also appointed me to this Commission. The programs of this agency were financed principally by the US Services Administration. We labored to put the unemployed into remunerative positions, put roofs over the heads of the indigent and the poor, and see that ethnic groups and women received the needed aid. We also opened an arts and crafts store for seniors. Elderly citizens who had hobbies brought their handicrafts to the store which tried to vend them to the public, the proceeds of course being remitted to the craft maker. The Brown Bag Program, which is now prevalent almost everywhere in the US, was the brainchild of this Commission. This innovative program started from donations from our growers/shippers, in the guise of boxes of vegetables, or in allowing our crew of seniors to cut vegetables from the fields. As other areas adopted the program, different sections traded their products with produce from other areas. As trading grew, the Brown Bag Program was able to distribute a greater variety of supplies. Brown Bag is
now a national program serving the needy, most of them seniors.

By law, I was forced to leave the Community Services Commission after almost six years of community service. But it did not end my social work with the county. A few weeks after I was released from this Commission, County Supervisor Shipnuck named me into the Drug and Alcoholic Advisory Committee. However, my associations with this group did not last the term of my appointment. The days and time needed to function fruitfully as a committee man conflicted with the days and my personal responsibilities in the American Legion. My services in the American Legion reached more people, so I opted to devote my time and efforts in serving them.

The Monterey County Affirmative Action Commission was my succeeding appointment for public service. I served this Commission for some five years, the term of service allowed by regulations. At every meeting, Department Directors were invited to present to us the affirmative action status of their departments. This allowed the Commissioners to know the status of the departments so that needed adjustments could be recommended.

On one occasion, the Director of Natividad Medical Center was our guest. He presented a good picture of his affirmative action program. This medical facility was one of the biggest employers in the County; and it was touted to be one of the best employers of ethnic races and women. Commissioners were not only allowed but required to ask questions to these Department heads, after the presentations. I personally knew that Natividad Hospital employed many Filipinos and I personally knew most of them. So I asked the Hospital Administrator a theory that was bothering me for eons of time. I pointed to him that Filipina nurses had been serving the medical facility for many years. They possessed the experiences, the expertise and the desire to work. I also mentioned that several them were holders of college degrees in nursing. My question was, "If affirmative action is duly applied, how come no Filipina nurse had been elevated to head nurse, yet some of your head nurses are just graduates of Hartnell College, two-year courses?"

His ready reply astounded me deeply. He said, "We have, and always have wanted to elevate these Filipina nurses. However, there has never been one who wished to accept the responsibilities."

Later, I asked several Filipina nurses at Natividad Medical Center to verify the truthfulness of the Medical Director to my question at the Commission's meeting. I was shocked by what I heard. It was a fact that Filipina nurses were recommended for promotion, but no one wished to accept the responsibility. They nonchalantly refused to accept because, they argued, the monetary price of the promotion did not equal the headaches and responsibilities that the position entailed.

Political And Community Service

The Monterey County Central Democratic Committee was another group with which I served. The Democrats in the county elected me twice to this political organization. However, due to the differences of persuasions and my belief of putting the welfare of the country above party affiliations, I had aroused the aggressions of other Commissioners. They did not hide their dislike of me, my politics, and my personality. To allow the committee to work harmoniously, I decided to resign my elective position.

It was evident from the start of my membership in this political group that I was not heartily welcomed. When I threw my hat into the Salinas City elections—running for city council in 1968[153]—not a single one endorsed me, although I was a sitting member on the committee. They never did mention my candidacy at our deliberations but when another colleague in the Central Committee ran for City Council in Pacific Grove, they spent hours of deliberations finding ways and means to have her elected. Ironic and discriminatory indeed!

In 1985, the Monterey County Grand Jury became my "grandest" exposure to the Democratic processes. The tenure of my grand jury panel lasted longer than any Grand Juries, past and present. Prior to our term, grand jurors served from July to June, exactly twelve months. That law was amended so that the term would be the calendar year, i.e., January to December. Ours then was unique—July to December the following year, a total of 18 months. The Education Committee of the Grand Jury was one into which I was assigned, and the Alisal School District became the principal focus of our committee.

We discovered numerous financial anomalies from the district administration. School funds were disbursed freely and for personal activities. Tours to Italy by the school superintendent and three associates were funded by school funds. Personal and group parties, featuring unlimited amounts of booze, were also financed by school money. School checks were carried out daily by personnel for ready and immediate use at their discretion. All of these inappropriate anomalies happened unhampered by the elected School Board. The superintendent and assistant and accountants (four of them) are still serving in California penitentiaries because of the investigation by our Grand Jury.[154]

The Monterey County Economic Committee was also a group to which my services were needed. The City of Salinas, Monterey County, also invited me to serve in volunteer services. The Neighborhood Betterment Committee was my first appointment. This group of citizens was charged with the task of studying how to improve the Alisal community, specifically the northside, East Market Street. Within blocks from the center of town, it was sticking out like a sore thumb. The city wanted our input as to how this section could be improved. Several plans, projects and possible changes were proposed, but it would require barrels full of expenditures. And the city was not prepared to meet the financial obligation. Limited improvements were made, yet the greater portion of the neighborhood is yet to be developed.

The Salinas City Mediation Board designed to solve differences between landlords and renters was also a program in which I devoted a lot of time. Board members were screened, tested, and given some training. We had to be knowledgeable with the rent-lease laws, the rights and responsibilities of the property owners, and the people who lived on the properties. My insignificant know-how as a real-estate broker and the training that the city imposed helped me greatly in executing my responsibility. Mediators worked in pairs, not necessarily the same personnel in the team as we worked when available. When a case was filed, mediators were called; those free would be assigned to the case to arrange meetings with those involved. I served in several interesting situations and succeeded also at arranging amicable agreement between the litigants. I derived great pleasure in giving my free time to this worthy program.

My next volunteer service with the City of Salinas was with the Affirmative Advisory Committee, which through our demands, was elevated by the City Council to the Affirmative

Commission. This group of citizens from all ethnic backgrounds participated actively in the recruitment of non-Anglos and women into city employment. We tried and succeeded in many cases to have non-Anglos selected to city employment. The highest point in my membership as an Affirmative Commissioner was my selection as one of five citizens who would pick the City of Salinas Chief of Police. It was a hard decision to make, especially when all five finalists were good people, experienced law enforcement officers from cities that faced similar problems as Salinas. The principal factor that finally made the screening committee unanimously choose our selection was his bilingualism and his years of working with Latinos here in the USA and in Mexico. I served in this committee for over five years, an experience and an education that made me understand more intimately people of different races.

I have heard it said that the wicked have no time to rest; they just jump from one hot seat to another. Truly, I had hoped to take a little breather, but my expectations were abruptly interrupted by the City Mayor, who then named me to the City Traffic and Transportation Commission. Commissioners served for the duration of the term of the appointing officer. My tenure was faced with the approval of the master plan of Salinas. We dealt with re-routing traffic, building new approaches to the city, and diverting congested traffic to other alternative routes. As funds were available, many traffic lights were installed within the city. Traffic and transportation is an unending problem of Salinas as it is in every fast-growing community. As a city grows, it attracts more people, more business, more homes, and more schools, and traffic remains an unending problem.

There were other government agencies that also considered my participation. The Superintendent of the Monterey County Office of Education, which needed to comply with sanctioned affirmative action directives, approached me directly to be part of a group to "start the ball rolling." At that time, I was active in the City and County Affirmative Action Commissions. I made myself available at their first session at the Monterey

County Office of Education. At that first meeting, it was unanimously agreed by those attending to comply with the consent decree and elect to become a working unit. There appeared no individual in the group who had actually worked for affirmative action, save myself. I found myself elected to handle the gavel, a position which I held for six succeeding years. We made some progress in placing minorities and women in positions within the Monterey County School Districts. However, I must admit with much regret our total failure to get men into the clerical world, a dilemma also encountered by other Affirmative Action Commissions. Clerical or office work will, I believe, remain the bastion of female domination.

There was abundant clamor by the overwhelming mass of Latinos that the voting system employed by Hartnell College[155] was discriminatory to them. The Hartnell College Board of Trustees was elected at large by voters within the College jurisdiction although each board member represented only a section of the whole spectrum. There were no Latinos ever elected to serve as College Trustee, so they demanded that the Board of Trustees should be elected by districts, a far-out alternate to the then at-large election by the united jurisdiction. A study was therefore instituted not only to determine the feasibility of the proposition but also to create boundaries between districts. I was one of those requested to serve this Ad Hoc Committee. We deliberated numerous times before we decided to submit our final recommendation. At present, the Hartnell College Board of Trustees is elected exclusively by their District's constituents. There are also districts whose populations are of majority Latinos, which translates into a more secure position by this clamoring ethnic group.

The Alisal Elementary School District in Salinas was once the workplace of the popular and much-admired School Superintendent, Virginia Barton. She never in any manner or form hesitated to gather the input of the parents and residents in the district. She requested and met with many parents and education-minded leaders in her district. She formed the Citizens Committee on Goals. Programs within the school district including budget became topics of study and discussions by the Committee of Concerned Parents and Citizens. The superintendent herself tapped me to join this Committee. We met at her option and discretion, especially when problems which were many and complex arose. I derived great pleasure and acquired vast learning experience serving the Alisal Elementary School District from which my sons began their pursuit for higher education.[156]

Service to the Filipino Community

As I had mentioned previously, the Filipino Community of Salinas Valley, organized in the fall of 1936, is an association I have served in many capacities. I was one of the original chapter members, serving as its first Vice-President, and have been a member from 1936 to 1995. I actively supported this group continuously, occupying the presidency for over ten years.[157]

The only break of my services occurred from 1990 to1993, when Perla Pigao was president. Pigao was someone I had helped rise to this high office. However, once she was president, my services were at her threshold but were adamantly refused. She went ungratefully to the extreme of denying me the floor at their meetings. One of our disagreements was propagated by the Urabe Park, adjacent to and behind the Filipino Community property. Initially, I was the first to start dialogue with the city—the mayor, the city attorney and the director of Parks and Recreation—for the purchase of the two-acre parcel. I learned from reliable sources that the Park became a liability to the city, so I visited City Hall requesting them to consider FCSV as an interested principal buyer. The two-acre parcel would be too expansive and expensive for the FCSV alone, so I also fostered an understanding with the priest of Christ the King Catholic Church, whose property was also adjacent to the park, to share in the purchase on a half-and-half basis. The purchase price was $200,000. The church agreed wholeheartedly to my proposal.

To finance the undertaking, I had conceived of a plan, which I presented to FCSV. When the City of Salinas was ready to negotiate the sale of Urabe Park, Pigao pulled me unceremoniously out of the negotiations. She took the "bull by the horns," completely ignoring my proposals and claiming them as irrelevant and unnecessary. She told the community members her own plans, and the non-thinking Board swallowed her policy—line and bait. I warned them that a bank loan was impossible, but the president claimed that three different banks were ready, willing, and able to finance the deal. Their borrowing proposal was denied, as I predicted, and we lost Urabe Park for good. The whole Urabe Park is now the property of Christ the King Church, developed into a parking lot, which at times, becomes available to FCSV for use, for a price indeed!

Under the same administration, an event occurred in which they tried to make me the "goat." At one of the membership meetings of FCSV, the lady with the gavel instructed one of her lieutenants to introduce a guest speaker on a subject that was supposedly for the good of the organization. The guest speaker was a local MD, Dr. Rudy Garcia, who turned out to be a regular member who could have just asked for the floor to air his views.

Dr. Rudy Garcia, whom I never met before that night, spent his entire discourse personally attacking, libeling, dishonoring me with the allegation that I voted against his application to renovate his house on East Market Street into a medical clinic and office. He pointed out to the group of Pigao idolizers that I—the only Filipino serving the City Traffic and Transportation Commission—opposed his application. Of course, I denied vigorously the accusation. Dr. Garcia had the wrong information. All ears—especially Pigao—refused to listen to me, the accused. In fact, they booed me, and the lady with the gavel concluded, "You heard Dr. Garcia speak. Manuel Luz, the only Filipino in the Traffic and Transportation Commission, voted against the doctor's application." In rage, she banged the gavel and stopped further mention of the case.

Three days elapsed. I visited City Hall to procure a copy of the minutes of our commission meeting which embodied the case of Dr. Garcia. The minutes clearly stated that I seconded the motion to accept his application. The minutes moreover clearly stated that I voted for the motion. My blood was boiling mad when I remembered that nobody believed me when I was uttering the whole truth and nothing but the whole truth. My first reaction was to sue the offending parties. I went to confer with my lawyer who assured me that the case would, without doubt, be decided in my favor. Before I told my lawyer to proceed, however, I showed the Commission minutes to a trusted friend, then a member of the FCSV Executive Board. He begged me not to act hastily and asked me to examine the status of the FCSV and consider the present and future of the organization. He pointed out to me that the FCSV had just recently undergone a lawsuit and that another court case would surely bleed and kill the association. He also begged me to agree to a meeting with the accuser, Dr. Garcia. He knew my deep feelings about the FCSV and he talked to me through that vein. I consented to confront the accuser.

My wife, who was madder that I, made sure that she was present at the meeting with Art Sabiniano, the friend acting as middleman. My wife, who was very hot under the collar, castigated the doctor who was very apologetic of his actions.[158] Realizing his grave mistake of not investigating and knowing the true facts before speaking, I dropped my plans to sue...with the premise that he make a public apology, and send copies of the written apology to all members of FCSV, which was implicitly carried out.

Dr. Garcia also initially told me that his informant was his building renovator. After his publicized apology, he admitted that his appearance to accuse me was motivated by the president and secretary who twice visited his home to arrange the orchestrated accusation.

My principal motivation not to go to court was this: I had

spent many years of hard-earned effort to see the FCSV grow, and given the precarious state of affairs, I knew that the suit would definitely kill the organization. The truth made me stand tall and I had the last laugh. My sole regret is knowing that the community, including its officers and members, though scared in shame, does not even now know how to admit the truth. Some manifested a change of heart, others were vocally mute, but some admit their mistakes. Most, however, simply dismiss the episode like it was a bad dream.[159]

The Fil-Visayan Association in America, a group dedicated to helping financially bereaved families of deceased members, is another Filipino group where I lavishly spent my time serving. I have served as a member and chairman of the Board of Directors for many years. I helped set up its existing bookkeeping system, a system praised by IRS accountants, who had examined them on a bi-yearly basis. I am presently enjoying the status of life member.

The Laoaguenians[160] is an association of which I was the principal organizer, and it has developed and grown into an influential body in local Filipino society. It has attracted many of the leaders, hopeful leaders, and the elite of the Filipino citizenry. It made me proud to see that its aim "Organized for Mutual Helpfulness" was generally adhered to.

There were other Filipino dubs or associations, pre-war or postwar, in which I had served officially and/or as an active member, whose ultimate goals were to seek, create and design beneficial programs for the Filipinos.[161] Those organizations faded out of existence by the draft of World War II, or had ended having accomplished their reasons for existence.

Service to the First and Second Filipino Regiments

In 1969, the former fighting soldiers of the First and Second Filipino Regiments[162] held a reunion in Monterey, California, under the initiative of a Major Turqueza. Most of the planning committee members were from Salinas, and although many attended from all over California, the Salinas delegation swelled the auditorium.

During many of our preparation meetings, I broached the proposition of establishing a permanent association of former members of the Filipino Regiments. The plan was heartily accepted and endorsed by all those attending. We therefore placed our dependence on the shoulders of leadership during their tour of duty as Army officers. There were Majors, Captains and Lieutenants in our midst; they were the ones the lowly soldiers relied on to receive orders from during their fighting days. They were the leaders; we were the lowly GIs looked to them to lead this organization. Many moons passed, but there appeared no action or sign of any desire by the former Army brass to initiate the organization.

The lowly GIs became restless—they were ripe to become active, working veterans of the Filipino Regiments Association. They eventually lost faith in our leaders of the war years, and many of them approached me—a lowly corporal who served with them for just a few months—and requested me to start the ball rolling and initiate the organization push.[163]

At that same period, I was buried with my responsibilities with the Filipino Community of Salinas Valley and in Fil-Am Post 652, The American Legion. But I felt that I could not refuse their pleadings and requests. So, I made reservations at the Filipino Community Hall at Lake Street[164] in Salinas. I also prepared a draft constitution and by-laws for the upcoming association. I then called upon those who pressured me so we could have our locomotive "choo-chooing" on the right track. The enthusiasm was high, so many interested ex-GIs eagerly attended. Among those attending were former Army brass—majors, captains and lieutenants. Without any opposition or hesitation, I wielded the gavel, and the meeting was called to order. The first action, as it was necessary, was to have a recorder of the entire proceedings. Alex Fabros, also an ex-NCO, was selected.

The first order of the day was to approve the formation of an organization composed of former personnel of the US Army

Filipino Regiments. The response was a thundering approval. It was also unanimously decided that the group would be named, "The First and Second Filipino Combat Infantry Regiments Association." The model constitution and by-laws that I personally prepared was presented, read, and discussed. The part that came under scrutiny were the titles of officers. My proposal was for military titles like Commander, Adjutant, Finance Officers, etc. My direction was based on the premise that since the organization would be composed of ex-GIs and military men, those titles would be appropriate and respectful. It also conformed to other working veteran organizations like the American Legion and the Veterans of Foreign Wars. The Filipino ex-GIs, however, preferred the more common terms of President, Vice-President, Secretary, etc. As a prelude to further actions, it was proposed and accepted to appoint a constitution and by-laws committee to further study and write a more detailed and comprehensive document with what had already been studied and discussed as the basic nucleus. The appointed committee was urged to perform their task as readily as time permitted, and to notify the president, Pro Tem, when they finished the polished product.

The alert committee wasted no time performing the task. Just a few weeks elapsed and the anticipated document was ready for the final scrutiny of the regimental veterans. I didn't hesitate to call another meeting.

At my beck and call, we assembled to finalize and adopt the supreme law of the First/Second Filipino Combat Infantry Regiments Association. The document with very minor changes was unanimously adopted. The Association therefore became a reality; all it needed were the leaders to launch and steer the new ship of state. I, without much ado with gavel in my hand, opened nominations for the positions as embodied in the by-laws. The nominations done, election followed. I, the lowly corporal, the President pro tem, was elected without opposition, as president. Elected and to serve as my Vice-President was Major Ruperto Sampayan, Secretary was Sgt. Alex Fabros and Treasurer was S/ Sgt. Johnny Albano. The other officers and Board of Directors were mostly enlisted men. The former Army officers declined or refused to serve, for reasons hard to comprehend.

Even before the pioneering officers of this embryo organization were officially installed, we rolled up their sleeves to lay a concrete foundation to withstand any and all sorts of catastrophic disasters. I chose the best and most willing members into permanent essential committees. The committees we deemed necessary were: Ways and Means, a financial group; Legislation, charged to watch proposed laws affecting the rights, privileges and responsibilities of the Veterans; and Community Service which was charged with the duties of what we could or could not do to serve the community we lived in. Consciously avowing that membership was not only the life blood of any working group, but also the strength, a Membership Committee was not ignored. With these committees on solid ground and officers and board members accepting their assignments with eagerness and enthusiasm, the new organization began to function smoothly forward.

One of the overwhelming and unanimous resolutions approved by the members was to sponsor and host a national reunion of the former personnel of the First/Second Filipino Regiments, US Army. Every member pledged his total support to this project; each one volunteered to work in a committee in which he felt comfortable and where he could contribute his very best. There was, however, a huge stumbling block to be hurdled. Former members of the Regiments were scattered all over the USA and some in foreign lands. How could we alert them? We didn't have addresses![165] This predicament was settled after I realized they could be reached through the medium of the press. As a Legionnaire, I succeeded in inserting an announcement about the scheduled reunion in the *American Legion Magazine*, a publication that graces over 2.5 million homes worldwide. The announcement served its purpose very well as evidenced by the many delegates who came to enjoy the comradeship.

Salinas, California, was the birthplace of the combat infantry regiments. So, for the first time ever, I was able to request the City Council of Salinas to declare the week of the reunion as First and Second Filipino Regiments Week. The reunion, which occurred on July 30 through August 1, 1971, was a three-day affair: Friday night was a welcome dance party at the Filipino Community Building for the delegates; Saturday was devoted to the muster of the troops at the Salinas Armory. Incredible but true. Every battalion and company in the Second Regiments was represented and designated by their own guidon! It was a sight to see these ex-GIs standing tall and proud to relive their patriotism in defending freedom, liberty, and democracy. Saturday night was the regimental ball, graced by a bevy of young beauties representing the different sectors of the fighting regiments. The following Sunday, an all-day barbecue at the Sheriff's Posse Grounds satisfied the discriminating tastes of everyone. The registration of delegates was a continuous activity during the three-day extravaganza.

To this day, no other reunion of the Filipino Veterans—and there have been countless numbers of them—was able to outshine, outdo or even stood in parity to that 1971 affair. It was an extravaganza cherished wholeheartedly by all in attendance.[166]

We did face a dilemma while we were planning the reunion. There was a clamor among the planners to have someone in the group deliver the keynote address. Most members placed their sights on their leaders in the battle fields; those who were imparting to them the orders that came from higher echelons. Even after repeated requests and pleadings, not one—I repeat, not one—even considered or had thoughts of accepting the task. When it was evident that our former brass would not consider tackling this assignment, the lowly ex-GIs had to pick one amongst them. To the surprise of everyone, there was not a single volunteer, even though some were leaders of other organizations. Their search then led to my door.

As the President, I had many duties to perform, numerous tasks to tackle, and plenty of responsibilities to accomplish. But they prevailed upon me to add another task to my busy schedule. The lowly corporal, who trained with them for only a few months,[167] was enlisted to deliver the keynote address. My time with the Regiments was limited to the training grounds in California. Their overseas activities were alien to me. I only knew what I read and heard from information from friends in the Regiments. Therefore, I was extremely leery if my keynote would hit the nail on the head.

I delivered the message during the muster of the troops. And I think I succeeded in my attempt, as evidenced by the thundering applause bursting in jubilation. Also, copies of my keynote address were requested by a number of the Anglo officers of the Regiments. As I had only one copy, it was given to the highest ranking officer present who promised to send copies to the others.

The First and Second Filipino Regiments Association grew into a working force in our Filipino society and became a model of achievement. After two fruitful years of stewardship, and despite the pressure to continue, I humbly surrendered my position as president. The demands of other commitments forced me to give way for others to lead. The members and other officers of the Regiments Association conferred upon me the Life Membership Award, in recognition of my "exemplary leadership" and accomplishments for two solid fruitful years. I remained the only Life Member until the fall of 1994 when others were awarded this honor. I, on several occasions, had suggested to the chairman of the executive board to consider granting this same award to my successor, who served for over two decades, but they saw no reason to accept my suggestion. However, at a meeting in 1994, the president suggested that Life Membership be awarded to more than a dozen followers. Those named had maintained their membership since day one of the organization. A motion was duly made to this effect by one of the named recipients and seconded by another.

The motion was approved, no doubt, because the quorum was predominantly the recipients who would not vote against themselves. Conflict of interest, no doubt, but incredibly made into fact. The President then included himself on the list and proclaimed himself the permanent president.

After my tenure as co-organizer and president and as time elapsed, the First and Second Filipino Regiments Association slowly but surely discarded the constitution and by-laws and shelved the original aims and objectives. These documents were put on the back burner, which are today unlit and sparkless. It is to my dismay that the association currently operates under the whims and thinking of the incumbent administrator, who does not consider the plight of the veterans, the disabled and those confined in beds or hospitals. Community services are no longer part of its agenda. Meetings at the beck and call of the "President for Life"[168] are dominated with information on the financial and social successes of himself and family members. Other issues at meetings concern the successes of the *Mahjong* parties regularly held at his residence. His birthday also became an integral part of the programs of the Association. It is indeed a transformation from service to personal aggrandizement—a move tantamount to a departure from the sublime to bordering the ridiculous. Those old soldiers who worked with might and soul in the Regiment's formation and have now faded away must feel betrayed by this discomforting turn of events.

Additional Community Service Croups

There are numerous community-oriented service groups where I gave my time and services without regrets. Some of these groups are enumerated herein:

Monterey County Veterans Credit Union. I served on the Board of Directors for many years, including service as Vice-President and President. I was one of the founding fathers. We served many soldiers, veterans, and their families and made loans to them—in the millions of dollars. This Credit Union finally merged with another credit union, and it is now called the First Credit Union of Monterey County.

The Monterey County Alliance on Aging. This group runs

nutrition sites in Monterey County, administers the Brown Bag Program, and performs numerous services to seniors, veterans and the needy. I, for many years, served on its Board of Directors.

Meals on Wheels. I served on the Board of Directors. We supplied and served shut-ins and impaired seniors, delivering hot meals every day. It also elated the hopes of those served by the visit, however short, by the food distributors.

Community Action Advisory Committee, California Employment Development Department. Members of this committee were charged with the responsibility of encouraging employers and employees to use this facility. At times, we served as members of groups screening job applicants. I fought for and succeeded in getting employment of Filipinos into this Department.[169]

Tri-County Affirmative Action Plan. The Tri-County Affirmative Action Plan (Counties of Monterey, Santa Cruz and San Benito) of the Building and Trades Industries was another entity which I served. I was chosen by and represented the Coalition of Japanese, Chinese, Filipinos and American Indians. This plan had a program to encouraged people to train in all phases of the building industry. Those interested were given extensive training from apprentices to masters of the trades. While in training, they performed compensatory work.

Saint Mary of the Nativity Catholic Church Council. I was a follower of Baha-Lullah (Bahai faith) when I lost my bachelor status in 1959. There was, however, no Bahai group in Monterey County at that time. The nearest of any Bahai community to my home was Santa Clara, a very inconvenient location for active participation. My wife was and is a very devoted Catholic. She could not miss Sunday masses or any Catholic sacred days. To show family unity, "a family that prays together stays together," I tagged along on her pilgrimages to her church. People noticed me regularly attend Sunday masses, so they assumed that I subscribed to Catholicism and accepted me as a believer. Through those circumstances, I, a non-Catholic, was elected by the congregation to the St. Mary of the Nativity Church Council. Incredible, indeed, but to serve my fellow men was and is my destiny. During my tenure, the Diocese of Monterey designed a program for raising funds especially earmarked for churches within the Diocese to finance improvements, priest's pensions, and other special plans. Father O'Halloran was the presiding priest and I represented St. Mary of the Nativity Church at the organizational meeting. The program continues annually, giving the Diocese of Monterey and the member parishes some needed income and a comfortable nest egg.

Salinas Chamber of Commerce Minority Advisory Board. It was also my privileged honor to have served in the Minority Advisory Board of the Salinas Chamber of Commerce. The City of Salinas in concert with the Chamber of Commerce sponsored the Congress for Community Progress. I was honored to be part of this resourceful project. I was tapped to serve as a panelist on the Human Resources Project.

Salinas Community Arts Council. The Salinas Community Arts Council and their annual International Cultural Day were other events where I was invited to participate. We Filipinos and the Filipino Community of Salinas Valley organization shared the days with exhibitions, dances, and *kundimans*.

Wee Explorers Day Care. The Wee Explorers Day Care in Salinas, California, was a non-profit corporation dedicated not just as a daycare but also as a school for the children. I was one of the incorporators and board member (now Vice-Chairman). Most, if not all of our employees are of Filipino extraction. Our charges, however, are a mixture of all races. All are equal—the color of skin or the shades of financial status are not considerations for the school. Wee Explorers is just one happy family.

ARAW. Arts, Research, Acculturation Workshop is a group dedicated to the propagation, expansion, and dissemination of Filipino culture among our children, and was in existence as a working group a decade ago. A *rondalla*[170] group was started (featuring mandolins, guitars and musical instruments brought in from the Philippines) with the children. They had public appearances in Salinas and elsewhere, gaining a reputation as a cultural body in demand. Singing groups, young and old, were also organized and developed. They were given public accolades in all their public appearances. For many years, I was a part of this organization, having served as a member of its board of directors. Unfortunately, the musical director, instructor, motivator—the power behind all these activities—faced some personal and immigration problems, and she, without choice, had to leave our city. No other person could be located to fill the vacuum left by her, and eventually the cultural group faded out of existence.

A Closing Note to My Community Service

I tried my best to use the prime times of my life to offer my services to my people and country. However, my sunset years are not totally devoid of further services. Educated in the school of hard knocks, wizened by the scars of experiences, toughened by indignities and discrimination, steeled by numerous misunderstandings and controversies, encouraged by the love and loyalty of my family, and with the divine guidance and blessings of my Creator, I am, at my age, enabled to further lend a helping hand.

Presently,[171] I am contributing my free services to the following tasks: Commander, Fil-Am Post #652, The American Legion; Chairman, Board of Directors, Fil-Visayan Association in America; Vice-Chairman, Board of Directors, Wee Explorers Day Care Center; Board Member, National Filipino American Council, Monterey County Chapter; Chairman, Board of Directors, The Laoaguenians; Parliamentarian, Special Member Board of Directors, Filipino Community of Salinas Valley; Advisor, Filipino Nurses Association of Central Coast, California.

If my health prevails, my services will be free at the public's disposal. So be it. Amen! Oh yes, the five dollars in change, though devaluated, is still preserved and intact...

---

[1] *See more on this in Chapter 4.*

[2] Author's Note: My attempt at becoming a lawyer was shut down by the laws of the State of California which did not allow me to take the bar examinations. At that time, Filipinos were not allowed by law to challenge the State Bar.

[3] Author's Note: In the Philippines, education sometimes appears more or less a hobby. You can count by the millions, the unemployed college graduates. In Laoag City, on the walls of most homes, are displayed college diplomas.

[4] *My brothers and I never met any of my father's original family, so we never met our uncles or aunts or grandparents. They were not only living far away from us, but they were also quite old. The exception is my older cousin, Editha, who immigrated to the United States as a teenager and helped care for me and my brother, Marcel,*

when we were toddlers. But being Filipino, we had many, many other "Uncles" and "Aunties" growing up!

[5] *A sundry or convenience store, usually family-run, and often-times, part of the family's home.*

[6] *This desire for higher education is universal to many Asian cultures, passed down to the generations in America as well. Education was a means upon which one could jump the social class structure.*

[7] *As a child, my dad was too old to participate in any sports with his sons. However, he was, to his dying days, a diehard New York Yankees fan.*

[8] *The values of hard-work, frugality, education, and pride—values which often come from first-generation immigrants—are born of such difficult beginnings. And of course, the values were very much instilled into all of the children, including myself.*

[9] *At our parents' insistence, all four sons received musical instruction. We all took piano lessons (though only Rhu and I kept at it), and we all were signed up to play in the school band or choir.*

[10] *The age of 18.*

[11] *According to the stories my dad told us, he literally missed the boat. He and his friend intended to work the fields in Hawaii and make enough money to afford tuition at the University in Manila, but when they arrived at the docks, the boat to Hawaii had already set sail. So they took the next boat, which as fate would have it, brought them to Seattle, Washington.*

[12] *General Artemio Ricarte was a Filipino general during the Philippine Revolution and the Philippines-American War of 1899 and is considered the Father of the modern Philippine Army.*

[13] *My father was 19 years of age when he arrived in Seattle.*

[14] Author's Note: It is important to note that many of those who favored armed participation escaped the draft, seeking refuge in the agricultural industry or in the defense industries. The others could have followed suit; yet they showed their undying love to their country by serving.

[15] *The First and Second Filipino Regiments provided more than 3,000 officers and enlisted men to the Pacific theater. These men, comprised of the many Filipino immigrants who arrived in the US during the 1920s-1930s, are regarded as some of the most decorated regimental units in World War II. Personnel won more than 50,000 decorations, awards, medals, ribbons, certificates, commendations, and citations. It is a point of pride that these men went back to their homeland to liberate it.*

[16] *When my dad married my mom, he dutifully attended Catholic mass every Sunday with his family.*

[17] *Just as a personal footnote, I just love how my dad described this as "manly cursing."*

[18] Author's Note: When I returned to civilian status, a number of people I knew told me how FBI agents pestered them for damaging causes against me.

[19] *A lot more on this fascinating, and life-defining, incident in Chapter 3.*

[20] Author's Note: After discharging from the Army, I had several encounters

with the disappearing soldier, and he swore that all his reports were favorable to my cause.

[21] Author's Note: Only 80,000 American soldiers of the over 2.5 million Armed Forces personnel were chosen for the ASTP. Everyone who was a soldier took the same IQ and mechanical aptitude tests, and from these tests, we were exclusively chosen, kept out of combat duty, and armed with the mighty pen, not with the gun. We had also passed intensive interviews by the Army brass and civilian trained interviewers. In essence, we were intellectuals kept out of combat duty to preserve brain power.

[22] Author's Note: After the cessation of hostilities of the war in the Pacific, and on my way for a vacation to the Philippines, I joined a guided tour of Tokyo and the vicinity, and I saw the definite spot of the much-acclaimed raid. There I saw with my own eyes the authenticity and validity of the journalist-lecturer expose.

[23] *"The Pearl of the Orient Seas" is a historical and romantic name for the Philippine Islands. My dad refers to his beloved homeland with this title several times in these memoirs.*

[24] *My dad was born and raised in the northern provincial capital city of Laoag, and hence spoke their local dialect, Ilocano. My mom was born and raised in the central provincial capital of Lucena City, and spoke Tagalog. At home, they spoke some Tagalog but mostly English for our benefit. As a result, my brothers and I are sadly monolingual, although we all know a few Tagalog swear words.*

[25] *At the age of 39 years old. While his service in the Army allowed him to receive his US citizenship, congress passed the Rescission Act of 1946, which disallowed the recognition of military service by Filipinos, essentially negating all veteran's benefits which should have been given them. Thus, they were denied disability compensation, veteran's pension programs, medical care through VA hospitals and medical facilities, education programs, housing and home loan guaranties, job training, small business loans, etc.*

[26] *As I mentioned, enlistment during the war allowed Filipino immigrants to have US citizenship. This opened the door to many other future rights and privileges, including land ownership, job opportunities, changes in marriage laws, and the like. And socially speaking, after the war, white Americans were generally more sympathetic to Filipinos, because they had fought together as allies.*

[27] *This was the same time as the great Okie Migration, also referred to as the Dust Bowl Migration. Faced with the Great Depression and a large and severe drought, farmers from Oklahoma, Missouri, Arkansas, and Texas relocated to California in search of work and a new beginning. Thus, a glut of workers, along with the down economy, created additional tensions in the fields. John Steinbeck's Grapes of Wrath tells this story well, but the story of the Filipino in this context has never truly been adequately told.*

[28] *United Cannery, Agricultural, Peanut and Allied Workers in America.*

[29] *American Federation of Labor, the precursor to today's AFL-CIO.*

[30] *Or as one Salinas Californian newspaper journalist called it, "the War in*

Salinas."

[31] *The Monterey Peninsula Herald did a feature on my dad decades later. Writer James Denison, in his July 12, 1981 article in the Herald wrote particularly about the War in Salinas and my dad's many encounters with bigotry. He wrote, "Community leader with a stormy past, Manuel L. Luz managed to win the toughest of all fights—the fight against discrimination."*

[32] *Recall in Chapter 2 the many issues my dad had in the military and why he was not granted assignments, promotions, and even a commission.*

[33] Author's Note: I was later informed that my qualifications overshadowed those of the employee who directed me to go thin lettuce.

[34] *Salinas was where my dad settled in 1935. He returned as a veteran and continued to make Salinas his home. And Salinas is where he met my mom and raised their family.*

[35] Author's Note: At that time, the Salinas office was a full-time operation which opened five days a week, eight hours a day.

[36] *For most of my childhood, a large, white, wooden sign hung at the front of our house, proclaiming "Manuel L. Luz, Real Estate-Insurance."*

[37] *On a more personal note, my dad's expertise in immigration law and procedure was the primary reason why my mom met Dad in 1959. Which of course led to my brother and me! More on this in Chapter 7.*

[38] *More on this in Chapter 9.*

[39] *As a young adult, I had a chance meeting with a correctional officer while waiting in line at a hardware store in Folsom, California. I could tell he was Filipino, and I casually mentioned that my father worked at Soledad Prison for many years when I was younger. When I mentioned his name, the officer lit up. He told me he had known Mr. Luz, and that he had encouraged him to apply for the job, which had then become his career.*

[40] *My dad worked as a correctional officer for 15 years.*

[41] *Just a few of the many organizations that my dad led over the course of his life. More in Chapters 6 and 9.*

[42] *My dad is playfully referring to my mom here. Cresencia Aranilla Luz served faithfully in the nursery at Memorial Hospital for 23 years before retiring (now renamed the Salinas Valley Memorial Healthcare System).*

[43] *My dad was involved in opening the door to the hiring of many Filipina nurses and other health care professionals.*

[44] Author's Note: "Black-balls" was a term usually given to those who shunned hard labor, especially field work.

[45] *See Notes 30 and 31.*

[46] *My father never talked about this period in his life to us. But in the few times it came up, there seemed to always be a sense of regret in his voice. Truly, my dad lived the life of the Prodigal Son (Luke 15:11-32) and spent the rest of his life living out his redemption.*

[47] *See the end of Chapter 2, as well as notes 25 and 26.*

[48] *The American Legion was an important part of my dad's life. I believe it was one of the first organizations that truly treated Filipinos like himself with equality and*

respect. He proudly served as founder, commander, and past commander locally, state-wide, and nationally at many gatherings and conventions.

[49] *This is covered in more detail in Chapter 9, My Community Service Involvement.*

[50] Author's Note: The Committee for the Protection of the Foreign Born was able to interest a New York congressman to introduce a resolution into the House of Representative to allow most foreign-born residents, including Filipinos, to file for American citizenship. Before World War II, most Filipinos, without much thought, rejected the idea, collectively believing that one would be a traitor to the homeland. The resolution was, however, rejected by the legislation.

[51] Author's Note: My Vice-President, Benny Espejo, later served as President. Under his leadership, the community building was erected. My treasurer, Phillip Ben, also served as President of the FCSV. Under his term, we accumulated enough cash to purchase the first lot owned by the association.

[52] *You may be wondering why it is a big deal that my dad points out the Chinatown connection. Here are his words: "Before and immediately after WW II, Chinatown in Salinas was the only zone in town where Filipinos could congregate freely. Businesses in that area thrived by the patronage of Filipinos. It was also unfortunately a zone of operation of discreet Chinese gambling dens, places where we, Filipinos, voluntarily habituated. Most of the hard-earned money of Filipinos were banked in these institutions. And all kinds of "sins" were rampant in this area. Therefore, it was not unusual to have crimes committed, many with Filipino involvement. It was also not unusual, indeed, to have Filipinos arrested or incarcerated. And it was not unusual that the majority of these felonies or misdemeanors stemmed from actions perpetuated by a Filipino against another Filipino or a Filipino gang against another gang. In many cases, I was called in by the police or by county judges with jurisdiction of the case, for assistance in the mitigation of the crime." So Chinatown had its reputation.*

[53] *President Woodrow Wilson had promised the Philippines independence after World War I, but Filipinos had to wait until the end of World War II before the Philippines became a self-governing nation.*

[54] *See note 48.*

[55] *William Taft was the first to coin the term, "Little brown brothers," to refer to the Filipino. It was not intended as a racial slur, but actually reflected the larger systemic racism related to American manifest destiny.*

[56] *Truly, the Filipino Community Hall was one of my father's greatest personal triumphs. It represented—to him and to many others—home. I have many fond memories of that building, including Christmas programs, recitals, dances, scholarship banquets, and even my Filipino wedding reception.*

[57] *It is a point of pride that, in my hometown of Salinas, California, it is pronounced "row-DAY-oh" and not "ROW-de-oh."*

[58] *Those who could trace their roots to the City of Laoag, capital of the northern province of Ilocos Norte, Philippines. My dad was a proud founding member of this organization.*

[59] *I myself was used as a boy to model some traditional Philippine children's clothing, and I remember seeing my picture in the local newspaper, the Salinas Californian!*
[60] *A formal long-sleeved translucent fabric shirt traditionally made from abaca or pineapple fiber. It is the national formal dress for men in the Philippines.*
[61] *A beautiful formal dress, typically with upright butterfly sleeves, worn by women. It is the national dress for women.*
[62] *A genre of traditional Filipino love songs.*
[63] *Similar to a Chinese egg roll, but usually includes pork, chicken, or seafood along with vegetables. Also tastes a hundred times better.*
[64] *A savory noodle dish with meat and vegetables enfolded in egg noodles, rice noodles, or a combination of both.*
[65] *I remember as a small child, piling into the station wagon with the family and going to the Filipino Community Hall to paint. I was a clumsy kid back then, and I remember backing into a large mirror, shattering it into a thousand pieces! Though my brothers gave me grief, I remember that my dad didn't get mad—he just made us clean it up.*
[66] *See the end of Chapter 3.*
[67] Author's Note: The beneficiary of a deceased registered member receives a benefit of $1,000.
[68] Author's Note: $3000 was given to scholarship recipients yearly, including two $1000 scholarships awarded to college students, and two $500 scholarships awarded to graduating high school students.
[69] Author's Note: A group which I organized and headed up.
[70] Author's Note: He still includes me in most of his visits to Salinas, as well as sending me greetings on my birthdays. And he sent me a get-well card when I was hospitalized.
[71] *Eventually, Burt Talcott was displaced by Leon Panetta, who went on to become Chief of Staff for President Bill Clinton.*
[72] Author's Note: This organization laboriously aided in the election of Ferdinand Marcos and Fernando Lopez as president and vice-president of the Republic of the Philippines, respectively.
[73] *See Service to the American Legion in Chapter 9.*
[74] *A copy of The Grapes of Wrath by John Steinbeck sat on the shelf in my dad's office for many, many years.*
[75] *City of Gonzales, California in 1965-1968.*
[76] *1975-1979.*
[77] *I remember being nine and sharing my dad's campaign flyers and cards with my fourth-grade class. While I obviously didn't understand the political and social and cultural repercussions, it was an exciting time for me personally, knowing that my dad, a brown-skinned Filipino, was involved in something significant.*
[78] *This caused quite a stir in Salinas at the time. As a child, I remember seeing a big photo of Dad in the local Salinas Californian newspaper—straw hat tipped above his head, a big Nixon headband displayed above the brim. I believe his public endorsement of Nixon, for better or for worse, was driven by conscience and not by*

politics. It was only later that the events of Watergate and Nixon's impeachment became clear.

[79] Author's Note: As a card-carrying democrat, no less!

[80] *My dad's work as an immigration specialist, as well as notary public, tax preparer, etc.*

[81] *See Chapter 9, Political and Community Service.*

[82] Author's Note: The many indiscretions of these school officials happened in 1984-1985.

[83] Author's Note: Atteridge honored me with an appointment to the Monterey County Community Services Commission.

[84] Author's Note: Shipnuck appointed me to the Community Services Commission and to the Alcohol and Drug Advisory Committee.

[85] Author's Note: Jeffries chose to appoint me into the City Traffic Transportation Commission after my over five years as a member of the City Affirmative Action Commission.

[86] *See previous note.*

[87] *A two-wheeled, horse-drawn carriage.*

[88] *When my dad passed in February of 2001, one of the things I inherited was a box of letters from a variety of women in the Philippines, all addressed to Dad. Though I've not read them, I have thought of publishing them, mostly as a way of documenting the isolated and often lonely life of the Manong generation in America.*

[89] *See Chapter 3 and Notes 39 and 40.*

[90] *Remember that it was only in the recent past that widespread lawful racism was practiced against the Filipino. For my dad to have a well-paying government job with benefits, be a homeowner, and also have a business on the side, made him an unusually accomplished, self-made Filipino American in 1959.*

[91] *See Chapter 3 and Note 37.*

[92] *Clothesline.*

[93] *My parents fussed often, but seldom argued. My dad did indeed wear the pants in the family, but my mom knew how to change his mind! More on this later in the chapter.*

[94] *Remember that this was before cell phones, and land lines, which were physically operated and connected by human beings, were the primary means of communication.*

[95] *My parents' anniversary is October 10, 1959, although they did get married a second time on December 28, 1982, in the Roman Catholic Church. My mom had been excommunicated from the church due to her divorce from her first husband in 1956 and had been recently reinstated into the church. Dad was hastily baptized that morning, and that same day, they were married, in the presence of their four adult sons, the immediate family, and some close friends. It was a memorable event.*

[96] Author's Note: Yearly schedules of vacations at Soledad Prison where I worked were usually arranged during the early part of the year. So there was no way to anticipate this turn of events.

[97] *My dad worked the early shift, 6:00 a.m. to 2:00 p.m., throughout his fifteen*

years at Soledad Prison.
[98] Author's Note: For years, I made my living working at restaurants and cafeterias.
[99] *My dad loved to tell this story, and I've personally heard it numerous times. The reality was that my mom, being the youngest in her family, never learned.*
[100] *Publications like The Philippines Mail were a vitally important part of the fabric of the Filipino culture during that time. This was where important issues, like immigration, politics, and unionization were discussed, as well as more personal issues like weddings and births and obituaries. These publications helped bring Filipinos together and gave them a sense of knowing and belonging.*
[101] Author's Note: I had occasionally served as a correspondent to The Philippines Mail, and at times, I actually served as a columnist and editor when Delfin went to the Philippines.
[102] *My brothers' names were initially anglicized to "Robert" and "Fred" although the former went back to his original name.*
[103] Author's Note: A few months following our marriage, Cres could no longer stand the "heat in the kitchen," as she craved to utilize her expertise as a registered nurse. She donned the immaculate white and practiced her profession for some twenty-five years in Salinas until she got burned out and finally retired.
[104] Author's Note: Manuel Jr. was younger than one year and Marcel was a newborn when this arrangement became operative.
[105] *See INS involvement in Chapter 3.*
[106] *See note 93.*
[107] *As a seven-year-old, I remember this episode of our lives vividly. Our mom packed everyone in the car and was ready to leave. But I decided that someone had to be home with my dad, so, against my mom's wishes, I refused to get in the car. I remember that moment being so unfair, thinking, "If I go, then no one will be with Dad." This broken family arrangement went a few days before my mom came over and, in an emotionally charged moment, fetched me.*
[108] *This was one of the worst times in my life. We had no friends, we didn't know the school or neighborhood, and our happy family had suddenly shattered. Being far advanced in my class, I had been accelerated from second to third grade this year. However, having moved to a ritzier Salinas school, I suddenly found myself being the dumbest kid in class. It felt petrifying, lonely, and hopeless.*
[109] Author's Note: She once visited a beautiful house with three cars better than our dilapidated junkers and personally found the refrigerator bare, with only a bottle of water within.
[110] *I remember near the end of the school year, waking up one weekend morning to discover my dad in bed with my mom. We didn't know what was happening, but we could tell that they were back together. We were so happy, Marcel and I were jumping on the bed!*
[111] *Obviously, the family dynamics growing up was complicated. Older father and displaced, divorced mother. Two older Filipino-raised children from a first marriage*

adjusting to life in America. Two little American-raised Filipino children learning their place. Four extremely rambunctious boys. And it is even more complicated now as adults. Maybe one day I'll write my memoirs too.

[112] *An antiquated term for grocery shopping.*

[113] My dad completed the writing of this book in 1995, so we've added to the clan since then. In addition to the boys, Debbie and I had twin girls, Rachel and Paige. Marcel and Davina had two more boys, Jonathan and Christopher. And Fred had a daughter with Brenda, Ariel. In total, Mom and Dad had fourteen grandchildren. And he lived long enough to see them all.

[114] *See my dad's story of becoming a correctional officer in Chapter 3.*

[115] *Fellow Filipino, countryman, or specifically townmate.*

[116] Author's Note: I was wearing the insignia of the 4th Air Force.

[117] *Pensionados were a particular category of Filipino immigrant. They were from the upper-class of Filipino society who came to the US on student visas to study abroad. They did not fraternize, nor did they identify with, the typical immigrant Filipino working in the fields or canneries, much in the same way they did not fraternize with their maids, gardeners, or house staff.*

[118] *A balikbayan is a Filipino returning to the Philippines, especially after having lived overseas.*

[119] *The Philippine Consulate is the government agency in charge of diplomatic relations, foreign travel, and the rights and welfare of Filipinos abroad.*

[120] Author's Note: The Philippine Consular Office had given me a letter of commendation for my generous assistance.

[121] *Sugar or honey.*

[122] *A person who merely follows orders, i.e., a servant.*

[123] Author's Note: No other third-class passengers were invited to the shindig.

[124] *See note 62.*

[125] Author's Note: We heard later that a couple of sick renegades were peeping through the window taking glimpses of the events in the luxury liner ballroom.

[126] Author's Note: I had personally helped many of them as requested to arrange their relocations.

[127] *Fare or fee.*

[128] *See note 118.*

[129] *See note 115.*

[130] *Filipino men in the 1940s-1950s prided themselves in their appearance. They wore the latest fads, dressed in hand-tailored suits and silk ties, and were quite style conscious, even if they were not financially well off. Also, I like that Dad refers to himself as "nattily dressed."*

[131] Author's Note: When I first arrived for my visit, my bags had been opened and displayed by my relatives. It happened that I brought my US Notary's Seal, and the crowd found it among my meager belongings. That started a rumor that I was a lawyer in America. The impression spread, and perhaps that was a

reason why, when I was watching court proceedings, the lawyers of the courtroom had their eyes on me.
[132] *See note 87.*
[133] Author's Note: Since then, I always prayed that whenever I took a trip elsewhere that no engine trouble should happen. Truly, I know nothing about mechanics!
[134] *Those who are from my dad's hometown, Laoag City, are called Laoaguenians.*
[135] *This quote sat quietly on the shelf above my dad's desk for many years.*
[136] *See note 52.*
[137] Author's Note: In movie theaters, Filipinos were allowed to occupy only a certain, undesirable nook in the room.
[138] Author's Note: American food could be had only in cafeterias in the neighborhood or at the Crystal Theater.
[139] *United Cannery Agricultural Peanut Workers of America.*
[140] *American Federation of Labor.*
[141] *Committee of Industrial Organizations.*
[142] Author's Note: In reality, they would not do the "stoop labor" that Filipino immigrants did.
[143] Author's Note: Note that in the mid-1930s, there were no bread lines open for Filipinos; neither did we have unemployment insurance or welfare services to help us.
[144] *See notes 25 and 26. In 1942, after the fall of Bataan and Corregidor to the Japanese, Congress passed a law which offered US citizenship to Filipinos and other nationalities who served in the armed forces.*
[145] Author's Note: Prior to World War II, I was a member of the Committee for the Protection of the Foreign Born and I campaigned for the passage of a House Resolution, sponsored by a New York Representative, to allow Filipinos and other nationals to become American citizens. Also see note 50.
[146] *Much more about my dad's immigration activities are detailed in Chapter 3.*
[147] Author's Note: From the time we received our post charter, I had been Commander for half of its existence. My last stint included the last four years (1991-1995) Where I functioned in every capacity the Constitution provided and required.

[148] White garrison cap designating my role as Department of California Vice-Commander or Area Commander.
[149] *If this hospital sounds familiar, it's because the Salinas Valley Memorial Hospital has been a part of the story for my whole life. My dad opened the door for Filipina health care workers there (see Chapter 3 and Notes 42 and 43). Mom worked there as a registered nurse (see Chapter 7 and Note 103). And both my brother, Marcel, my favorite cousins, Arlene and Eric, and I were born there, in the same second floor nursery that Mom worked at for 25 years.*
[150] *When my dad had heart problems in his later years, he ended up in the SVMH Heart Center, the same place he had been raising campaign funds for.*
[151] Author's Note: I was recommended to follow the Afro-American candi-

date, but I readily declined in favor of the Latino candidate. I did not relish the idea of unpopular unacceptance by the Hispanic population there.

[152] Author's Note: Only a handful of Filipinos and other Asians were beneficiaries of this project. The gospel truth is that they never ask and never demand. They just work hard and help themselves.

[153] *See Chapter 6 and Note 77.*

[154] *See Notes 81 and 82.*

[155] *The only community college in Salinas.*

[156] *My three brothers and I all attended Bardin Elementary School in the Alisal Elementary School District.*

[157] *See Chapter 5, The Filipino Community Connection.*

[158] *On a personal note, I can just imagine my mom, a registered nurse, finally getting the chance to dress down a doctor. I bet it was epic.*

[159] Author's Note: I keep wondering how these people, who idolized their "dynamic president," Perla Pigao, feel now that the truth came out and she is out of office. Indeed, they are now out of sight, and the FCSV is left in a deep pit of unmet bills.

[160] *See note 58.*

[161] Author's Note: I, Manuel L. Luz, a controversial person, past and present, remain a misunderstood figure.

[162] *See note 15.*

[163] Authors note: Well, Napoleon and Hitler were corporals; Benedict Arnold was a General.

[164] *In later years, the City of Salinas became sister cities with Cebu City, in the Province of Cebu, Philippines, and Lake Street (where the Filipino Community Hall was located) was ceremoniously renamed "Calle Cebu."*

[165] *Remember, this was 1969. No internet, no email, no texting, no Google.*

[166] *This gathering was a quarter century after the regiments were disbanded. In that 25 years, one can only imagine the scope of social and political changes that had occurred for first-generation Filipino immigrants. They were now able to obtain citizenship, vote, get good paying jobs, and date and marry without fear of retaliation. They had fought for the American dream, and now they had the opportunity to chase it. I can just imagine what that evening must have felt like.*

[167] Author's Note: I had been separated from them to serve in the US Army Military Intelligence Corps (see Chapter 2).

[168] Authors Note: The vice-president was never allowed to preside on a session, even when the President was indisposed or unavailable.

[169] *This is mentioned in more detail in Chapter 3.*

[170] *A musical ensemble of native Filipino stringed instruments, usually playing traditional music.*

[171] *These memoirs were completed in May 1995, six years before Dad's passing.*

www.ingramcontent.com/pod-product-compliance
Ingram Content Group UK Ltd.
Pitfield, Milton Keynes, MK11 3LW, UK
UKHW021909190726
13853UKWH00002B/584